American Birding Association

Field Guide

to Birds of

Ontario

Chris Earley

PHOTOGRAPHS BY
Brian E. Small
AND OTHERS

Scott & Nix, Inc.
NEW YORK

To Todd, Joel, and Kashawehgo, a friend in need is a friend indeed. Thank you so much.

A SCOTT & NIX EDITION

COPYRIGHT © 2023 BY CHRIS EARLEY AND SCOTT & NIX, INC.
ALL RIGHTS RESERVED.

PUBLISHED BY SCOTT & NIX, INC.
150 W 28TH ST, STE 1900
NEW YORK, NY 10001
SCOTTANDNIX.COM

FIRST EDITION 2023

ISBN 978-1-935622-76-5

AMERICAN BIRDING ASSOCIATION®
AND ITS LOGO ARE REGISTERED TRADEMARKS OF
THE AMERICAN BIRDING ASSOCIATION, INC.
ALL RIGHTS RESERVED.

AMERICAN BIRDING ASSOCIATION, INC.
800-850-2473
ABA.ORG

SCOTT & NIX, INC. BOOKS
ARE DISTRIBUTED TO THE TRADE BY

INDEPENDENT PUBLISHERS GROUP (IPG)
814 NORTH FRANKLIN STREET
CHICAGO, IL 60610
800-888-4741
IPGBOOK.COM

PRINTED IN CHINA THROUGH PORTER PRINT GROUP, BETHESDA, MARYLAND

THE PAPER OF THIS BOOK IS FSC CERTIFIED, WHICH
ASSURES IT WAS MADE FROM WELL MANAGED FORESTS
AND OTHER CONTROLLED SOURCES.

Contents

**american birding
association**

The American Birding Association inspires all people to enjoy and protect wild birds.

The ABA represents the North American birding community and supports birders through publications, conferences, workshops, events, partnerships, and networks.

The ABA's education programs promote birding skills, ornithological knowledge, and the development of and implementation of a conservation ethic.

The ABA encourages birders to apply their skills to help conserve birds and their habitats, and we represent the interests of birders in planning and legislative arenas.

We welcome all birders as members.

**THE AMERICAN BIRDING ASSOCIATION
CODE OF ETHICS**

1. Respect and promote birds and their environment.

(a) Support the conservation of birds and their habitats. Engage in and promote bird-friendly practices whenever possible, such as keeping cats and other domestic animals indoors or controlled, acting to prevent window strikes, maintaining safe feeding stations, landscaping with native plants, drinking shade-grown coffee, and advocating for conservation policies. Be mindful of any negative environmental impacts of your activities, including contributing to climate change. Reduce or offset such impacts as much as you are able.

(b) Avoid stressing birds or exposing them to danger. Be particularly cautious around active nests and nesting colonies, roosts, display sites, and feeding sites. Limit the use of recordings and other audio methods of attracting birds, particularly in heavily birded areas, for species that are rare in the area, and for species that are threatened or endangered. Always exercise caution and restraint when photographing, recording, or otherwise approaching birds.

(c) Always minimize habitat disturbance. Consider the benefits of staying on trails, preserving snags, and similar practices.

2. **Respect and promote the birding community and its individual members.**

(a) Be an exemplary ethical role model by following this Code and leading by example. Always bird and report with honesty and integrity.

(b) Respect the interests, rights, and skill levels of fellow birders, as well as people participating in other outdoor activities. Freely share your knowledge and experience and be especially helpful to beginning birders.

(c) Share bird observations freely, provided such reporting would not violate other sections of this Code, as birders, ornithologists, and conservationists derive considerable benefit from publicly available bird sightings.

(d) Approach instances of perceived unethical birding behavior with sensitivity and respect; try to resolve the matter in a positive manner, keeping in mind that perspectives vary. Use the situation as an opportunity to teach by example and to introduce more people to this Code.

(e) In group birding situations, promote knowledge by everyone in the group of the practices in this Code and ensure that the group does not unduly interfere with others using the same area.

3. **Respect and promote the law and the rights of others.**

(a) Never enter private property without the landowner's permission. Respect the interests of and interact positively with people living in the area where you are birding.

(b) Familiarize yourself with and follow all laws, rules,

and regulations governing activities at your birding location. In particular, be aware of regulations related to birds, such as disturbance of protected nesting areas or sensitive habitats, and the use of audio or food lures. Everyone who enjoys birds and birding must always respect wildlife, its environment, and the rights of others. In any conflict of interest between birds and birders, the welfare of the birds and their environment comes first.

Birding should be fun and help build a better future for birds, for birders, and for all people

Birds and birding opportunities are shared resources that should be open and accessible to all

Birders should always give back more than they take

Foreword

I am so happy to share with you the first American Birding
Association bird guide to a Canadian province! This is a long-
awaited addition to the ABA series of state/provincial guides.
Ontario is one of the most exciting places to bird in North America
and with shorelines along four of the Great Lakes, James Bay, and
Hudson Bay, and habitats varying from temperate forests to tundra,
there is quite a variety of species to entice any birder.

Like all the guides in this series, this book can help you explore as
much as you want about Ontario's birds. For those curious about
birds in your neighborhood and local parks, this book provides a
solid foundation for learning and discovery. For those looking to
take a plunge into the great diversity of year-round and breeding
species of Ontario, your journey can start in this book. Our aim is to
meet you where you are and give you useful, reliable information
and insight into birds and birding. Chris Earley, who is the
Interpretive Biologist and Education Coordinator at the University
of Guelph Arboretum, is author of a dozen other books about birds
and nature. His knowledge and years of sharing birds with others
makes him an excellent and seasoned guide to profile Ontario's
birds. Longtime ABA contributor, Brian Small, and other talented
photographers have captured the key features of identification in
their photographs while conveying the utter beauty of each bird.

I invite you to visit the American Birding Association website (aba.
org), where you'll find a wealth of free resources and ways to
connect with the birding community that will help you get the most
from your birding in Ontario and beyond. Please consider becoming
an ABA member yourself—one of the best parts of birding is joining
a community of fun, passionate people.

If you're like me, the best part of exploring a new field guide is
flipping through and getting a feel for what you're about to
discover. Don't let me hold you up—dive in!

Good birding to you,

Nikki Belmonte, *Executive Director*
American Birding Association

Birds in Ontario

Welcome to birding in Ontario! You are certainly in the right spot to see lots of different birds. As of June 2022, the official tally of species recorded in the province was 508 species.

This diversity is due mostly to the immense size of Ontario, more than one and a half times that of Texas. Ontario also spans a huge range of latitudes. Pelee Island in Lake Erie is farther south than the northern border of California, while the northwestern corner of the province is at the same latitude as the halfway point of the Alaska Panhandle. The expanse between north and south allows Ontario to have a wide range of habitats and to be home to the following four forest regions.

DECIDUOUS FOREST OR CAROLINIAN ZONE

This is the southernmost and warmest region. Located in a thin band along the north shores of Lakes Erie and Ontario, it is home to more species at risk than any other forest in Canada, and its bird species composition is similar to that of the forests of the eastern United States.

In 1994, the Common Loon became the official provincial bird of Ontario. Its haunting calls symbolize the vast wilderness areas of the province.

GREAT LAKES-SAINT LAWRENCE FOREST

This mixed forest crosses southern and central Ontario, reaching west from the shore of Lake Superior and east from Lakes Superior and Huron to the Saint Lawrence River. The second largest forest region in the province, it is where most Ontarians live, yet the diversity of breeding bird species in the spring and summer is still high.

BOREAL FOREST

Part of an immense swath of forest that spans the whole country, this mostly coniferous habitat covers 50 percent of the province's area and supports a staggering number of birds.

HUDSON BAY LOWLANDS

Made up of forest, wetlands, and tundra, this is the northern-most forest region. Located between the Canadian Shield and the south shores of Hudson Bay and James Bay and covering more than a quarter of Ontario's area, it is used by breeding and migratory boreal and Arctic species.

Within these zones are also found the shorelines of the world's biggest freshwater lakes (four of five Great Lakes); thousands of forest-edged lakes, rivers, and bogs; the Arctic Ocean; remnant prairies; and limestone escarpments, as well as farmland and urban centres.

The secretive Canada Warbler prefers to nest in forests with a dense understory,

Birding Year

Drastic seasonal fluctuations mean that the presence and abundance of certain species in Ontario change throughout the year. Here is a brief description of the birds you might find in each month. (Keep in mind that, depending on your location in the province, arrivals and departures may occur earlier or later.)

JANUARY The height of winter and usually our snowiest month but still a great time for birding. In years when northern birds irrupt, or move southward, Boreal Owls, Northern Hawk Owls, and Great Gray Owls are found, and winter finches and Bohemian Waxwings irrupt as well. In areas where the Great Lakes haven't frozen over, concentrations of ducks occur. January is also a good time to watch the behaviour of common species at feeders, which might also attract Cooper's Hawks, Sharp-shinned Hawks, Northern Goshawks, and other predators, as well as the occasional rarity.

FEBRUARY Winter continues its hold. Snowy Owls are present in numbers that vary from year to year, and open fields attract large flocks of Snow Buntings—remember to search each flock carefully for Lapland Longspurs. Horned Larks may join in as well. At the end of the month, early migrants start to trickle in,

The majestic Great Gray Owl is on the wish list of many birders.

and sightings of Red-winged Blackbirds, Common Grackles, and Brown-headed Cowbirds increase.

MARCH This fickle month can either announce spring or drone on about winter. As such, which birds are found in March varies greatly from year to year. Song Sparrows return to many areas, regardless of the weather, and Mourning Doves, American Robins, and Black-capped Chickadees start to sing in earnest. The sounds of Killdeer and Tundra Swans are also heard. Depending on conditions, duck numbers increase as areas of open water become larger.

APRIL Migration really begins. Many more species are present. Ruby-crowned Kinglets sing their jumbled songs everywhere by mid-month. At night, wet fields and scrub become communal display areas, or leks, for the American Woodcock. Many raptors move north to re-establish territories, and ducks, loons, grebes, and other waterfowl appear on small lakes throughout the province that have lost their ice. Eastern Phoebes collect flies on sunny building walls, and Eastern Bluebirds check out nest boxes, while Canada Geese are already sitting on nests.

MAY Migration is at its peak, and birds are everywhere. Colourful warblers steal the show, but vireos, thrushes, flycatchers, Rose-breasted Grosbeaks, Indigo Buntings,

Eastern Bluebirds are a favourite species of open areas and farm field hedgerows.

Baltimore Orioles, and Scarlet Tanagers grab your eye, too. Mudflats, wet fields, and sewage lagoons attract shorebirds. Mid-month is when birders take an extra-long weekend or two to visit migration hot spots and be immersed in birdy goodness.

JUNE Nesting time. The woods are loud with song, as territories must be defended at all costs. Birding by ear becomes especially important, as full leaf-out makes relying on your eyes alone much more difficult. Songbirds carry material for building nests or food for hungry nestlings. Believe it or not, by the end of the month, some Lesser Yellowlegs start to migrate south.

JULY Fledging time. Feeders become busier, as parents bring their flying young to the smorgasbord. American Goldfinches that have waited for certain seeds to mature start to nest, and more shorebirds arrive on their southward journeys.

AUGUST Ontario's quietest birding month. Common Loons are still caring for their now-large chicks, but not for long. Shorebirds continue to pass through. And early migrants move south. Adult songbirds that have made it through the breeding season show up in non-breeding plumage before migrating or settling in for a long winter stay.

SEPTEMBER Small-bird migration is much more spread out in

Adult Lesser Yellowlegs who have failed in their northern breeding attempts start migrating south in early summer.

fall than in spring, but departing warblers, vireos, and flycatchers make some days surprisingly busy. Massive numbers of Broad-winged Hawks move with other raptor species along the north shore of Lake Erie. Numbers of Broad-wingeds peak in the middle of the month, while highest hawk diversity occurs towards the end. Ducks show up in large numbers, and easterly winds start to push jaegers and other pelagic rarities to the west shore of Lake Ontario.

OCTOBER Raptor migration continues, many different species of sparrow move through, and northern breeders such as the American Tree Sparrow and Dark-eyed Junco return to southern feeding stations. Late-migrating warblers are seen, including the Orange-crowned and Yellow-rumped Warblers, along with both Ruby-crowned and Golden-crowned Kinglets.

NOVEMBER By the middle of the month, you can pull on your long underwear and join birders along the Niagara River to see how many gull species you can find in the throngs of Bonaparte's, Ring-billed, and Herring Gulls. (The world record, set here, is 14 species in one day.) While in the area, watch for Black Vultures, Red-throated Loons, Tufted Titmice, and ducks. November is also the best month for spotting Golden Eagles gliding along the north shore of Lake Erie.

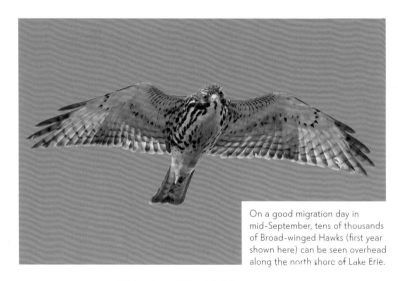

On a good migration day in mid-September, tens of thousands of Broad-winged Hawks (first year shown here) can be seen overhead along the north shore of Lake Erie.

DECEMBER The first of the month marks the start of the winter birding season, which ends February 28 (29). Keeping a bird list during the shortest days of the year is a popular pastime among Ontario birders. Christmas Bird Counts take place after the middle of the month, including some for kids. By participating in this long-standing citizen science project, not only will you (and your children) generate valuable data, but you will also meet local birders who may become companions on birding expeditions in the new year.

Birding Locations

There are too many excellent birding spots across Ontario to list here. The accompanying chart highlights just a few of the best places that you will want to visit.

SITE	SEASON	BIRDS
Algonquin Provincial Park	All year	Breeding forest birds, winter finches, Canada Jay, Spruce Grouse
Amherst Island	Winter	Owls, hawks
Beamer Memorial Conservation Area	Spring	Migrant raptors
Bruce Peninsula	All year	Migrant and breeding songbirds, overwintering hawks and Snowy Owl, grassland birds, Piping Plover
Carden Alvar	Spring-fall	Migrant and breeding songbirds, grassland birds, Yellow Rail, Loggerhead Shrike
Hamilton Harbour	Fall-spring	Gulls, jaegers, waterfowl, migrant songbirds, Trumpeter Swan
Hillman Marsh Conservation Area	Spring-fall	Migrant waterfowl, shorebirds, gulls, herons, marsh birds
Holiday Beach	Fall	Migrant raptors, marsh birds, waterfowl

Lake Saint Clair	Spring-fall	Marsh birds, migrant waterfowl, Yellow-headed Blackbird
Long Point	All year	Migrant and breeding songbirds, waterfowl, marsh birds, Sandhill Crane
Moosonee	Summer-fall	Boreal birds, migrant shorebirds
Niagara River	Late fall-winter	Gulls, waterfowl, Black Vulture
Ottawa River and Lac Deschênes	Fall-spring	Waterfowl, shorebirds, Barrow's Goldeneye
Pelee Island	Spring-fall	Migrant songbirds
Pinery Provincial Park	Spring-fall	Migrant and breeding songbirds
Point Pelee National Park	Spring-fall	Migrant songbirds
Prince Edward County	Fall-spring	Migrant songbirds, waterfowl
Rainy River	Spring-fall	Western birds, boreal birds
Rondeau Provincial Park	Spring-fall	Waterfowl, migrant and breeding songbirds, marsh birds, Prothonotary Warbler
Thunder Bay	All year	Boreal birds, migrants, Gyrfalcon
Tommy Thompson Park (Leslie Street Spit)	Fall-spring	Migrant songbirds, waterfowl
Wheatley Provincial Park	Spring	Migrant songbirds

How to Use This Book

The goal of this guide is not to describe all 508 bird species on the official Ontario checklist but to introduce you to the birds that are seen in the province most regularly. You might be lucky enough to spot a species that is not treated here. In that case, the Ontario Bird Records Committee, the keeper of the official provincial record, might ask you to submit a written description of your sighting, along with any photos, video, or drawings that support it. Check the checklist in the back of the book to see which species require such a report.

This field guide generally presents only a few images for each species. This is enough to portray most birds, but individuals in a few groups, such as gulls, appear in many different plumages in their lifetimes, more than can be covered here. Please refer to more detailed guides to learn how to recognize these seasonal and age- and sex-related plumage variations.

Each account gives a bird's common name in English and French as well as its scientific name in italics. The bird's length (L) and wingspan (WS) are noted, and an introductory paragraph describes an aspect of the bird's life or identification challenges. Where relevant, each bird's most commonly heard vocalizations are also described. Key field marks are addressed in photo captions.

In general, species appear in the order of the American Birding Association checklist, which is based on the authoritative list produced by the American Ornithological Society. The exceptions are a few species that were displaced to put similar-looking species together or to accommodate the layout of the book.

Bird Identification 101

In addition to behavioural clues and sounds, this section examines five groups of birds—warblers and vireos, hawks and falcons, ducks, gulls, and shorebirds—to help you learn the parts of a bird as well as the terminology used to describe field marks and shapes. Getting to know bird topography is key to remembering the field marks that are crucial to identifying birds, and having a mental checklist of things to look for will assist you, especially if your observation is fleeting.

WARBLERS AND VIREOS

These small birds can be challenging to learn not only because they're often hard to see as they flit through the leaves overhead, but also because there are so many field marks to keep track of. Learning ahead of time what to look for when you're in the field is very helpful.

Warblers and vireos are not closely related. Warblers are genetically closer to sparrows and tanagers, while vireos are more closely related to jays and shrikes. However, many warblers and vireos fill similar ecological niches and are often found in the same areas. Overall, vireos are chunkier and slower moving, and they have a small hook at the end of their beak that may be visible if you get a really good look.

Here's a checklist of field marks to check to identify warblers and vireos:

THROAT COLOUR Many similar-looking species can be differentiated instantly by their throat colour. For example, both the Magnolia Warbler and the Yellow-rumped Warbler are a combination of yellow, black, white, and gray, but seeing their throats instantly separates them.

HEAD PATTERN This field mark has a mini-checklist of its own: Does your bird have an eye ring? If so, is it thick or thin or broken? Does the bird have an eyebrow (strong, faint, yellow, white)? Does the eyebrow combine with an eye ring to make "spectacles"? Is an eye line present? Is it strong or faint? Does the head have a cheek patch, a moustache, sideburns, a cap, a crown stripe?

UNDERPARTS These include the breast, belly, flanks, and the so-called undertail coverts, the feathers that overlap the base of the tail. Noticing the colour of the undertail coverts can be very important, especially for duller, confusing species. As well, note the presence of markings such as streaks, spots, bands, or colour patches.

WINGBARS The presence or absence of wingbars is a key feature in this group. Some warblers have a wing patch instead.

TAIL SPOTS When a bird folds its tail feathers together, the outermost feathers end up at the bottom of the stack, and white or yellowish areas in them form characteristic patterns that are visible on the underside of the tail. Like wingbars, the presence, absence, and shape of these tail spots can help to identify warblers.

As well, note that the outer tail feathers of some other species may be all white, making them contrast with the inner tail feathers. This can be a very good identification feature, especially when a bird is in flight.

• • •

The next two pages (xxiv–xxv) highlight the diversity of field marks and their locations on various species of warbler and vireo.

Blue-headed Vireo

Northern Parula

Louisiana Waterthrush

Blue-winged Warbler

Yellow-throated Vireo

Blackburnian Warbler

tail spots

Blackpoll Warbler

short tail spots

Magnolia Warbler

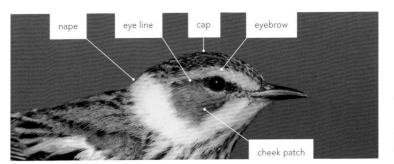

nape

eye line

cap

eyebrow

cheek patch

Cape May Warbler

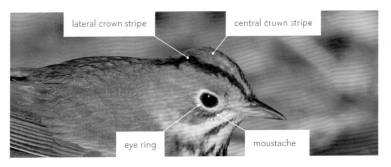

lateral crown stripe

central crown stripe

eye ring

moustache

Ovenbird

HAWKS AND FALCONS

Hawks and falcons are another pair that are not closely related—falcons hold more genetic affinities with parrots than they do with hawks. But the birds fill similar niches and, as birds of prey, can be similar in shape and markings. Getting to know what they look like in flight is especially important.

Here's checklist of features to help identify hawks and falcons:.

OVERALL SHAPE Knowing how a hawk or falcon flies can help you recognize it. For example, a Red-tailed Hawk in a full soar (wings held wide open) has rounded wingtips, while one cutting through the sky in a glide will show pointed wingtips. And if the hawk is diving in a stoop to grab prey, its wings will be mostly tucked in. Other clues to watch for are the length of the tail and wings. How the wings are held is telling, too: Does the bird hold them in a V shape over the back? Does the head protrude markedly in front of the leading edge of the wings?

DISTINCTIVE MARKINGS Luckily, most markings don't change with how the wings are held. Watch for "wrist" patches and comma-shaped markings on the underside of the wings, barring, "windows" (primary feathers that are paler than the nearby secondary feathers), and, on Red-tailed Hawks, so-called patagial marks, or dark patches on the leading edge of the wing close to the body.

TAIL PATTERN This can be especially helpful when watching hawks and falcons. Look at tail barring carefully. Are the pale bars the same thickness as the dark bars? Are the bars thin or thick? Is the tip a different colour?

comma

underwing coverts

leading edge

wrist

primaries

patagial mark

secondaries

undertail coverts

belly band

trailing edge

Red-tailed Hawk

This Golden Eagle is soaring with its wings fully extended and its primary feathers and tail fully spread. This allows the bird to catch as much air as possible and to circle with little effort.

This Northern Harrier is gliding. Its black primary tips are folded, making the wing look pointier than usual. Its tail is also folded. This posture allows the bird to cut quickly through the air or to move forwards in strong winds.

The Merlin has a thick-thin tail pattern of thick black bands and thin white bands.

The Osprey has many thin bands on its tail.

A thick black band separates the rufous tail of the male American Kestrel from the white band at the tip. The outer tail feathers are white and spotted.

DUCKS

Wing patterns can help with distant ducks, especially tricky females. Sometimes parts of patterns can be glimpsed while a bird is swimming, but it's when the duck stretches its wings or starts to fly that you really get to see the full pattern. Is the colour most noticeable in the so-called speculum (a patch of colour on the secondary feathers) or on the shoulder? Where is the white on the upper wing?

shoulder · back · beak · speculum · tail · breast · throat · chin · secondaries · Northern Shoveler · primaries

primaries · shoulder · crown · breast · undertail coverts · flank · Northern Shoveler

GULLS

Identifying most adult gulls is all about the wing tips. The presence and location of black, grey, and/or white on the tips of the primaries can help distinguish gulls. As well, the colour of the mantle is very important, as are overall size and eye and leg colour.

Get to know the gulls you see regularly—the Ring-billed, Herring, and Bonaparte's Gulls—really well, so you can compare them to other species. You should note, for instance, whether an unfamiliar gull standing near a Ring-billed Gull is bigger or smaller than the Ring-billed, or if it has a slightly darker mantle, and if a mystery gull flying beside a Herring Gull has as an equal amount of black in its wingtips. Once you get to know the adults, then you can start figuring out the immature gulls.

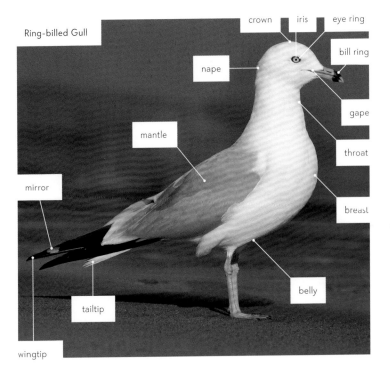

Ring-billed Gull

crown · iris · eye ring · bill ring · nape · gape · throat · mantle · breast · mirror · belly · tailtip · wingtip

SHOREBIRDS

Considering that these birds are out in the open most of the time, it's surprising that shorebirds such as sandpipers and plovers can be so difficult to identify. Shape is very important. Study leg length, beak length, beak shape, body shape, and neck length. In these photos, compare shapes and lengths. Differences in beak shape can be very subtle. Don't worry if they are confusing at first. Practice, practice, practice!

The Semipalmated Sandpiper is a small and compact sandpiper with a short straight beak. Its head is largish for its size.

Can you see how the medium-length beak of this Dunlin has a slightly drooping tip?

The Greater Yellowlegs has long legs, a long neck, and a longish beak that is slightly upturned.

BEHAVIOURAL CLUES

While it is natural to look first for field marks, always note how a bird moves or behaves. Behaviours are distinctive; they will help you identify birds.

American Kestrels, Eastern Phoebes, and Palm Warblers, for instance, pump their tails constantly. Spotted Sandpipers and both waterthrushes bob their rear ends as they forage along the water's edge. Connecticut Warblers, unlike most other warblers, don't hop; they walk. Swans, geese, coots, gallinules, and dabbling ducks such as Mallards and Northern Pintalls do most of their feeding at the water's surface, while loons, grebes, cormorants, and diving ducks such as mergansers and scaup dive under water to find their food.

Learning how each bird moves and behaves takes time but will make identifications faster and easier.

SOUNDS

Many of the accounts in this guide describe songs or calls that you might hear. But written descriptions are never as good as listening to a recording. Be sure to use online resources, such as Dendroica (www.natureinstruct.org/dendroica), xeno-canto

The Eastern Phoebe is our only flycatcher that pumps its tail.

(xeno-canto.org), and the Cornell Lab of Ornithology's Macaulay Library (www.macaulaylibrary.org).

A good birding app can be very helpful in the field. The Sibley Birds and Larkwire apps include many different songs and calls for each species and are wonderful tools for testing yourself as you learn. As well, virtual or in-person workshops are excellent ways to learn how to remember bird sounds. You can also double-check your identifications by using the Cornell Lab's free Merlin Bird ID app, which allows you to record and identify what you hear.

All in all, though, the best way to learn a new sound is to find the bird making it and watch it sing or call. Combining the visual and auditory information right in the field will help your brain remember which species makes which sound.

Keep in mind that, for most people, learning sounds is usually harder than learning what each bird looks like. Be patient with yourself. Add sounds to your repertoire slowly. And don't worry if, after one spring of learning songs, the next spring you have forgotten everything. It happens to all of us. Over the years, the length of time required for a song to click back in place will become shorter and shorter.

A Clay-colored Sparrow belts out its distinctive buzzy song.

CAN'T IDENTIFY THE BIRD?

No worries! While identifying a bird is terrific, not knowing what it is shouldn't stop you from enjoying the bird itself. Study how it feeds, builds its nest, or preens. While you are watching, you are still gathering information. Chances are, the next time you see that species, you might notice something you missed the last time, and, voilà, you've figured it out!

It is important not to get frustrated or to expect too much from yourself. No one expects you to learn how to identify all the birds instantly. Enjoy the birds you see, and be thankful that you can connect to our natural world!

Additional Resources

Ontario birders are a very friendly bunch, and most are more than happy to help a new birder with an identification. If you are struggling with an odd gull, a female duck, or a distant shorebird, ask nearby birders for help. They will always be your best resource in the field. Listed below are additional resources that are highly recommended for use at home, either after your outing or while you're planning your next one:

The Sibley Guide to Birds, Second Edition, by David Allen Sibley: This is many birders' favourite guide to North America's birds, but certainly not the only one. Peruse a few guides before you decide which one might be best for you.

Atlas of the Breeding Birds of Ontario 2001–2005, edited by Michael D. Cadman, Donald A. Sutherland, Gregor G. Beck, Denis Lepage, and Andrew R. Couturier: This large detailed book presents information gathered during the first and second breeding bird atlases about birds that breed in Ontario. Note: A third atlas is underway, so a new resource will soon follow.

Best Places to Bird in Ontario, by Kenneth Burrell and Michael Burrell: If you want help finding birds in Ontario, this is the book for you. It gives details about birding hot spots and the birds that could be found there. It is organized into regions so you can plan your route to different places in a certain area

125 Nature Hot Spots in Ontario: The Best Parks, Conservation Areas and Wild Places, by Chris Earley and Tracy C. Read: This guide highlights places that have many different natural features and wildlife (including birds) that you might want to see. If family members or friends are less into birding than you but still enjoy the outdoors, this book provides ideas about where to go with them.

Feed the Birds: Attract and Identify 196 Common North American Birds, by Chris Earley: How to use a bird feeder to learn to identify and study backyard birds.

Warblers of the Great Lakes Region and Eastern North America, Sparrows and Finches of the Great Lakes Region and Eastern North America, Hawks and Owls of Eastern North America, and *Waterfowl of Eastern North America*, by Chris Earley: These four photographic guides (with photos from Brian E. Small and many of the other photographers whose work illustrates this book) delve into the details of identifying and learning about birds in each group.

Ontario Field Ornithologists (www.ofo.ca): This large and supportive group enhances every aspect of birding in Ontario. It organizes tours, conducts and publishes research, compiles rare bird records, and keeps the province's official checklist. I strongly encourage you to become a member, so you can learn from, and get involved with, the wonderful work it does.

eBird (ebird.org): This website and app are the best way to keep track of your bird sightings. As a bonus, your sightings may contribute to vital bird research—you will become a part of citizen science. Most amazing is how eBird enables you to learn which birds have been seen in your area recently and discover great places to search for them.

American Birding Association

Field Guide
to Birds
of Ontario

Snow Goose
Oie des neiges
Anser caerulescens

L 69–83 CM (27–33 IN) | **WS** 138 CM (54.5 IN)

In flight, a flock of these well-named birds can look like a flurry of giant snowflakes. And often interspersed in the snowstorm are dark, or "blue," individuals that were considered a separate species up to 1983. One of the best places to see large collections of Snow Geese during their fall and spring migrations is along the Saint Lawrence River. Thousands of honking birds can sometimes be found in the agricultural fields between Morrisburg and Cornwall, southeast of Ottawa. When they take off, it's a treat for the ears as well as the eyes. In other places in southern Ontario, Snow Geese are more likely to show up as individuals in flocks of migrating Canada Geese.

White-morph adult all white with black wing tips. Beak pink with black "lips." (First-winter geese greyish with dusky beak and legs. Faint eye line.)

Blue-morph adult all dark with white head, belly, and undertail coverts. Light wing linings seen in flight. (White-morph adult all white with black primaries.)

Ross's Goose

Oie de ross

Anser rossii

L 59-64 CM (23-25 IN) | **WS** 113-116 CM (44.5-45.5 IN)

The Ross's Goose is an uncommon to rare migrant in Ontario, although sightings have become more common since breeding populations increased in the eastern Arctic and the goose started nesting in the Hudson Bay Lowlands in the mid-1970s. The Ross's Goose looks like a diminutive version of the Snow Goose. It has the white plumage, black wing tips, and pink beak of its larger cousin. It even has a rare blue morph, though some think this might be due to hybridization with a blue-phase Snow Goose. But the Ross's Goose lacks the black "lips" of the Snow Goose, and it's much smaller and more compact, although size can be hard to judge unless other waterfowl are around for comparison. Gives a high-pitched yelp.

Small. Adult all white with black wing tips, short neck, and pink beak with no black "lips." (First-winter geese greyer with dusky feet and legs. Faint eye line.)

Adult all white with black primaries.

Greater White-fronted Goose

Oie rieuse

Anser albifrons

L 64–81 CM (25–32 IN) | **WS** 135 CM (53 IN)

During its long migrations to its Arctic breeding grounds, the Greater White-fronted Goose makes fewer stops than many other waterfowl species. This means that seeing one is more difficult, so it is always a good idea to scan carefully through flocks of migratory Canada Geese, just in case a few Greater White-fronted Geese are among them. But be careful: more than one birder has misidentified an escaped domestic Graylag-type Goose as a Greater White-fronted Goose. Domestic geese tend to be much plumper, often have more white sections in their body plumage, and may lack the Greater White-fronted Goose's white flank stripe. The Greater White-fronted Goose's call is a laughing *loo-laa-luck*.

Brown body with white undertail coverts and white stripe on flank. Beak pink with white patch around base. Legs orange.

In flight, note black blotches on belly.

Brant

Bernache cravant

Branta bernicla

L 60–62 CM (23.5–24.5 IN) | **WS** 105–108 CM (41.5–42.5 IN)

These small, ocean-loving Arctic geese are about the same
length as Mallards but heavier, and they're very fast; some have
been recorded flying over 80 km/h (49.7 mph). Brant prefer
to feed on eelgrass, a coastal plant, so they have not taken to
foraging on commercial grains, as many other goose species
have. The Ottawa area may host flocks of migrating Brant near
the Ottawa River, and parts of Lake Ontario can attract them as
well. While Brant don't nest in Ontario, they feed and congre-
gate in James Bay in the Hudson Bay Lowlands, an important
gathering (or staging) place for the species during migration.
Call is a low *ronk*.

Small goose with black head,
neck, and breast and thin white
patch on side of throat. Back and
wings brownish grey. Underparts
lighter. White undertail coverts
and rump. Short black beak and
dark legs. In flight, note short
neck and tail.

Cackling Goose

Bernache de hutchins

Branta hutchinsii

L 63–65 cm (25–25.5 in) | **WS** 108–111 cm (42.5–43.5 in)

Before the Cackling Goose was split from the Canada Goose, in 2004, the Canada Goose had the widest range of body sizes of any bird species in the world, from 1.6 kg (3.5 lbs) to 4.9 kg (10.8 lbs). Now the Cackling Goose covers much of the lighter end of this spectrum. And while it is much rarer in Ontario than the ubiquitous Canada Goose, and usually much smaller, identification can still be tricky, since Canada Geese can vary in body size, neck length, and beak length. The Cackling Goose gets its name from its high-pitched cackling call.

Small, with brown body and white undertail coverts. Head and neck black with white cheek patch. Neck and beak short.

Canada Goose

Bernache du Canada

Branta canadensis

L 76–110 CM (30–43.5 IN) | **WS** 127–170 CM (50–67 IN)

Many people have a love/hate relationship with Canada Geese.
They love watching the birds migrate across the sky in V forma-
tions but hate dodging goose poop. Considering how abundant
and widespread Canada Geese are, it's surprising to learn
that the species was extirpated from southern Ontario until
reintroduction efforts began in the early 1900s. Now Canada
Geese are year-round residents in most cities and towns in the
southern parts of the province, often attracted to the monocul-
ture of lawn habitat. Call is a loud *uh-ronk*, made by males, and
a higher-pitched *uh-rink*, given by females.

In flight, note how white
undertail coverts contrast
with rest of plumage.

Large, with brown body and
white undertail coverts. Head
and neck black with white
cheek patch. Long neck and
large beak.

Trumpeter Swan

Cygne trompette

Cygnus buccinator

L 138–158 CM (54.5–62 IN) | **WS** 203 CM (80 IN)

Weighing 10.4 kg (23 lbs), the Trumpeter Swan is one of the heaviest flying birds in the world. Unfortunately, its massive size also made it one of the best targets for hunters. By the early 1900s, it seemed doomed to extinction. But thanks to conservation efforts and a reintroduction program, the species is now making a slow but sure comeback. The best place to see Trumpeters in Ontario is LaSalle Park in Burlington, where many overwinter. Compared to the Tundra Swan, the Trumpeter's call is more of a trumpet-like honk, sounding more like a crane than a goose.

Adult all white and huge, with long neck and large black beak. Forehead pointed where it meets top of beak. May have yellowish staining on head and neck. (White primaries show in flight.) First-winter swan washed with dusky grey. May have some pink on beak.

Tundra Swan

Cygne siffleur

Cygnus columbianus

L 120–147 CM (47–58 IN) | **WS** 168 CM (66 IN)

Canada Geese were once the harbingers of spring for many Ontario residents, but today's resident population makes this less apparent, so Tundra Swans now furnish the needed announcement. Thousands stop in southern Ontario on their 6,000 km (3,728 mi) trip from their wintering area in Chesapeake Bay on the Atlantic coast to their breeding area in the Mackenzie Delta of the Northwest Territories. The large white birds often blanket open fields along the route. One of the largest concentrations can be found at the Aylmer Wildlife Management Area. It is definitely worth a visit in March to experience the swans before they continue on their way. Call is a bark-like *who* that sounds more like a goose than a crane.

In flight, note white primaries, not black, as on Snow Goose. Adult all white and large, with large black beak and variable amount of yellow between eye and beak. Forehead rounded where it meets beak. May have yellowish staining on head and neck.

Mute Swan

Cygne tuberculé

Cygnus olor

L 127–152 CM (50–60 IN) | **WS** 208–238 CM (82–93.5 IN)

Introduced to many places in North America since the mid-1800s, the aggressive Mute Swan does not tolerate native waterfowl in its territory. When an introduced species has negative effects on native species, it is deemed invasive. It remains to be seen what the full effects of this species could be on recovering populations of Trumpeter Swans. Approximately 3,000 Mute Swans are in the lower Great Lakes area of Ontario. Though quieter than other swans, they are not mute; they produce hisses, grunts, snorts, and a feeble honk.

Adult all white and large. Large orange beak with black knob. Sometimes holds neck curved. First-fall swan (inset) may be dusky. Pink instead of orange on beak.

Wood Duck

Canard branchu

Aix sponsa

L 47-54 CM (18.5-21.5 IN) | **WS** 66-73 CM (26-29 IN)

Once hunted until it was quite rare, the Wood Duck today is the beneficiary of recent conservation efforts across North America. Its recovery represents a success story that will hopefully help other endangered species in the future. Probably the most colourful bird in Ontario, it is a duck of woodlands. It lays its eggs in hollow trees and old nest cavities of Pileated Woodpeckers, and acorns are a regular part of its diet. The male produces a squeaky whistle, the female a loud *oooeeeeek!*, often given when she takes off.

Male has red eye and red beak marked with black and white. Green and purplish head has crest with white borders. Throat white. Tail long.

Female has dark beak and white eye ring/patch. Head crested. Throat white. Body mostly brown with some iridescence on wings. Tail long.

Blue-winged Teal

Sarcelle à ailes bleues

Spatula discors

L 36–41 CM (14–16 IN) | **WS** 56–62 CM (22–24.5 IN)

Identifying female ducks can be a challenge. Many are brown and mottled, with little obvious markings to show who is who. Luckily, when a female Blue-winged Teal takes off, she reveals a giant patch of grey-blue on her wing. The only other common Ontario duck to have that same patch is the Northern Shoveler, which is distinguished by its long, spoon-shaped beak. Most Blue-winged Teal don't arrive in Ontario until April and usually leave by October, giving them one of the shortest seasons of a waterfowl species in the province. The male makes high-pitched whistles or chirps, and the female gives a high-pitched quack.

Male has purplish-grey head with white crescent between eye and beak and conspicuous blue shoulder and green speculum. Undertail coverts and rump black. White patch on rear flank.

Female has dark beak, often light patch at base of beak, dark eye line, and mottled brown body. Conceals green speculum and/or blue shoulder when swimming. Legs yellowish.

Northern Shoveler

Canard souchet

Spatula clypeata

L 44–51 CM (17.5–20 IN) | **WS** 69–84 CM (27–31 IN)

The Northern Shoveler's massive beak is an adaptation to its special feeding niche. Mallards, American Black Ducks, and other dabbling ducks feed by moving water through tiny projections called lamellae along the sides of their beaks. The lamellae work like the baleen of giant whales: they sieve out invertebrates from the water. The Northern Shoveler's lamellae are especially dense, allowing them to filter out very small invertebrates that are often in more open water. Consequently, Northern Shovelers may feed in the middle of ponds, rather than along the edges, like other dabbling duck species. The female has a low-pitched, often two-part, hollow quack.

Blue shoulders and green speculum seen in flight. (Female's shoulders more greyish.)

Adult has very long, wide beak. Male has green head with black beak and yellow eye, white breast, and chestnut flanks. Female mottled brown. Beak orange with mottling.

Gadwall

Canard chipeau

Mareca strepera

L 46–57 CM (18–22.5 IN) | **WS** 84 CM (33 IN)

Most male dabbling ducks have bright green heads, long tails, blue wings, rusty flanks, or other colourful adornments, but not the male Gadwall. As a result, he may be overlooked as he swims amid a mixed flock on a spring pond. A close look, however, will reveal finely detailed breast and flank patterns, making him rather dapper. The duck's white speculum and the male's black rump also help with identification. Females give a harsh quack.

Male with light head and dark beak. Breast dark grey with herringbone pattern. Undertail coverts and rump black. In flight, note chestnut wing patch (not present on female) and white speculum.

Female has orange beak with mottling and steep forehead. White speculum often concealed when swimming.

American Wigeon

Canard d'Amérique

Mareca americana

L 42-59 CM (16.5-23 IN) | **WS** 84 CM (33 IN)

This duck is a pirate. It likes to eat plants that grow in water too deep for it to reach. So, instead of diving, it hangs around with Canvasbacks, Redheads, Lesser Scaup, and American Coots and grabs the greens they bring to the surface, earning it the nickname "poacher." If plundering plants isn't an option, the American Wigeon, unlike other ducks, uses its stout beak to graze on grasses like a goose. The male's grey and green head and white crown distinguish it from its rare cousin, the Eurasian Wigeon, which has a chestnut head with a buffy crown. The male American Wigeon makes a three- or four-part rubber duck-like whistle. The female gives a harsh, low, piratelike *errrrr*.

Male has green patch behind eye, white forehead and crown, and speckled cheek. Beak light grey with black border. White shoulder may show as small patch on swimming bird. White patch on rear flank and black undertail coverts.

Female has speckled head with steep forehead. Beak light grey with black border. Body mottled brown, richer brown on flanks.

Mallard

Canard colvert

Anas platyrhynchos

L 50-65 CM (20-25.5 IN) | **WS** 82-95 CM (32.5-37.5 IN)

When a bird is as common as the Mallard, it is easy to overlook, but both the male and the female deserve attention, not only because they're gorgeous but also because they are incredibly adaptable, equally at home in wetlands, suburban backyards, and city streets. They allow us to watch courtship and nesting behaviour up close. And time spent studying Mallards, especially the females, will help you identify other ducks. The male gives a raspy *reeb*. The female makes a loud quack.

Male with green head and yellow beak, white neck ring, chestnut breast, grey flanks, and black undertail coverts and rump. Blue speculum with white border seen in flight.

Female is mottled brown. Head paler, with dark eye line and orange beak with mottling. Tail whitish. Blue speculum with white border seen in flight but often concealed when swimming.

American Black Duck

Canard noir

Anas rubripes

L 54–59 CM (21.5–23 IN) | **WS** 88–95 CM (34.5–37.5 IN)

The American Black Duck and the Mallard are so closely related that they frequently hybridize. Mallards were once more common in the prairies, but with the clearing of eastern forests, they moved into the American Black Duck's former range. American Black Ducks are forest ducks, and their populations have been dropping for decades, likely due to habitat loss, though hybridization may also be playing a role. Many male hybrids are fairly easy to spot; they look like American Black Ducks with green patches on the sides of their heads. Males give a raspy *reeb*, and females make a loud quack.

In flight, note purplish-blue speculum bordered with black. White wing linings contrast with belly.

Dark brown. Head paler, with dark eye line. Beak dull yellow (male) shown here or dusky green (female).

Northern Pintail
Canard pilet
Anas acuta

L 51-76 CM (20-30 IN) | **WS** 86.5 CM (34 IN)

The graceful-looking Northern Pintail is a welcome sight
on any waterfowl-viewing excursion. The female shares the
mottled brown of most other female dabbling ducks, but her
elegant neck and pointed tail are distinctive. The Northern
Pintail has had one of the biggest declines of any duck species
since the 1970s; almost half of the North American population has been lost. Its breeding range is spotty across southern
Ontario and almost non-existent in the boreal region, but the
ducks occur as breeders in the Hudson Bay Lowlands. The male
gives a high-pitched nasally call and a double whistle. The
females makes a soft quack.

Male has brown head, slender white neck, and
grey and black beak. Sides grey with white or
buffy patch on rear flank. Undertail coverts
black. Central tail feathers long and black.

Female mottled brown with
slender neck and dark beak. No
or indistinct eye line. Pointed tail.

Green-winged Teal

Sarcelle d'hiver

Anas crecca

L 31–39 CM (12–15.5 IN) | **WS** 52–59 CM (20.5–23 IN)

Shape provides an important clue for distinguishing dabbling ducks, and especially for identifying the females. The female Green-winged Teal is stocky, more compact than the similarly sized female Blue-winged Teal, and she has a steeper forehead. In addition, Green-winged Teal have very fast wingbeats and fly in tight flocks that twist and turn in synchrony. The male gives a spring peeper-like whistle, while the female makes a high-pitched, raspy quack, sometimes given in a descending series.

Male has large chestnut head with green patch behind eye and white crescent on grey flank. Yellow patch beside black undertail coverts. Legs grey or yellowish.

Small. Female is mottled brown with steep forehead and indistinct eye line. Legs grey. Green speculum often concealed when swimming.

Canvasback
Fuligule à dos blanc
Aythya valisineria

L 48–56 CM (19–22 IN) | **WS** 79–89 CM (31–35 IN)

The Canvasback, a large diving duck, is a favourite of birders because, even at a distance, its distinctive doorstop-shaped head helps with identification. The head of the similar Redhead is more rounded, and it also has a more colourful bill. The Canvasback gets its species name *valisineria* from the wild celery (genus *Vallisneria*), one of its favourite foods. The duck nests in only a handful of places in Ontario, including Walpole Island on the northern edge of Lake Saint Clair. The female can make a low growl.

Male has wedge-shaped, reddish-chestnut head with red eyes and black beak. Breast black. Back and flanks greyish white. Undertail coverts and rump black.

Female has brown head and breast. Note wedge-shaped head. Beak black. Indistinct whitish eye line. Back and flanks brownish grey.

Redhead
Fuligule à tête rouge
Aythya americana

L 42-54 CM (16.5-21.5 IN) | **WS** 75-79 CM (29.5-31 IN)

Redhead nesting is complicated. The female chooses one of three strategies each breeding season: (1) She builds a nest and incubates her own clutch, (2) she lays early eggs in other ducks' nests and then builds a nest and incubates a clutch herself, or (3) she lays all her eggs in the nests of other ducks. She can switch her strategy each season, depending on the breeding conditions, and sometimes she makes mistakes: Redheads have been recorded laying eggs in the nests of American Bitterns and Northern Harriers. Nesting occurs patchily across the province, usually in large marshes along the edges of big lakes and rivers. Females can make a growling squawk.

Male has reddish-chestnut head, yellow eyes, and grey beak with white and black tip. Breast black, back and flanks grey, and undertail coverts and rump black.

Female has brown head and body. Beak grey with faint white and black tip. Indistinct whitish eye line and eye ring.

Greater Scaup

Fuligule milouinan

Aythya marila

L 39–56 CM (15.5–22 IN) | **WS** 72–79 CM (28.5–31 IN)

Distinguishing Greater and Lesser Scaup can be challenging. Head shape plays an important role in getting the identification correct, but birds can change their head shape depending on their mood, so it might not be possible to identify every scaup you see. If you find a female with ducklings in southern Ontario, she is likely a Lesser Scaup, since Greater Scaup nest much farther north in the Hudson Bay Lowlands. Female makes a low growl.

Male has black head with greenish (or sometimes purplish) sheen. Head rounded; highest point often in front of eye. Beak large and grey with black tip. Breast black, back grey, flanks white, and undertail coverts and rump black.

Female has brown head and breast with variably sized white patch at base of beak. Beak large and grey with black tip. May have whitish ear patch. Back and flanks greyish brown.

Lesser Scaup

Petit Fuligule

Aythya affinis

L 39-46 CM (15.5-18 IN) | **WS** 68-78 CM (27-31 IN)

Because Greater and Lesser Scaup look so similar, even scientists have trouble getting accurate population counts. Often they have to lump the species together into a category labeled "scaup." To help with identification, go through this list: (1) head shape, (2) male head colour, (3) beak size, (4) wing stripe in flight (on Lesser, the stripe is bright white in the secondaries only, while on Greater, it extends into the primaries), and (5) overall size. If other birders are nearby, be sure to ask their opinions, too. Female gives a low growl.

Male has black head with purplish (or sometimes green) sheen. Head peaked; highest point often behind eye. Beak grey with black tip. Breast black, back grey, flanks white or light grey, and undertail coverts and rump black.

Female has brown head and breast with variably sized white patch at base of beak. Beak grey with black tip. May have whitish ear patch. Back and flanks greyish brown.

Ring-necked Duck

Fuligule à collier

Aythya collaris

L 39–46 cm (15.5–18 in) | **WS** 62–63 cm (24.5–25 in)

This lovely duck was named for the hard-to-see rusty collar around its neck; the name "ring-billed duck" might be more appropriate. It breeds in shallow wetlands, such as marshes and bogs, and can be found nesting across much of Ontario except the southwest. During his courtship display, the male may throw back his head until it touches his back and/or swim forward while nodding his head forwards and backwards. Like many other displaying duck species, he may also preen behind his open wing. Female may give a soft growl.

Male has peaked black head with purplish sheen. Beak grey with white outline and ring. Breast, back, rump, and undertail coverts black. Flanks grey with whitish crescents near breast.

Female brown with peaked head. Brownish-grey cheeks give bird capped appearance. Variable white at base of beak. Eye ring and eye line white. White ring on grey beak.

Harlequin Duck

Arlequin plongeur
Histrionicus histrionicus

L 34–46 CM (13.5–18 IN) | **WS** 56–66 CM (22–26 IN)

The Harlequin Duck prefers clear, fast-flowing rivers of northeastern and northwestern North America and is a rare visitor to Ontario's Great Lakes or large rivers. Therefore, it is worth going to see when it shows up, especially to observe the colours of the male. His slate-grey body is covered in spots and patches of chestnut and white; this patchwork pattern is where the name "harlequin" comes from. The female looks similar to a female Bufflehead but has more spots on her head. There are no Ontario breeding records for the Harlequin Duck. Males squeak, and females have a harsh quack.

Male has dark bluish-grey head and body. Face marked with white crescent, chestnut lateral crown stripe, and white spot and stripe behind eye. White stripe on neck, side of breast, and above chestnut flanks. White spot on side of undertail coverts.

Female brown. Irregular white patch at base of beak. White spot behind eye.

King Eider
Eider à tête grise
Somateria spectabilis
L 50-70 cm (20-28 in) **WS** 86-102 cm (34-40 in)

The male King Eider is quite the spectacle. But be warned:
when one of these northern ducks shows up in the Great Lakes
area, it is usually a female or first-winter male. Any eider is
interesting to see, however, because its boxy head and weird
beak are so strangely shaped. The best place to look for one in
southern Ontario is among the large rafts of ducks that float off
the shores of Lake Ontario from late fall to early spring.

Breeding male has bluish-grey cap and
nape, greenish cheek, and orange beak with
large, black-bordered, orange-yellow knob.
Two black "shark fins" not always visible.

First-winter male variable. Usually brown. Beak with
small orange knob. Throat and breast mottled
white. Female (below) mottled brown with black
beak and possible indistinct eye line and eye ring.
Flanks show sideways V shapes.

Long-tailed Duck

Harelde kakawi

Clangula hyemalis

L 40-47 CM (16-18.5 IN) | **WS** 71-72 CM (28-28.5 IN)

The Long-tailed Duck has many different plumages. In summer, its head is dark and it has a white patch on the face, but in winter, the head is white with a dark face patch. The winter plumage is easy to see in Ontario, as Long-tailed Ducks are found in this season at various places on the Great Lakes and the Niagara and Saint Clair Rivers. In summer, the duck nests in the far northern edges of the Hudson Bay Lowlands. The male gives a loud *ooo-squawak* yodel, sometimes heard in flight. The female has a low quack.

Winter male has white head and neck and large grey and black cheek patch. Beak black and pink. Upper breast white; lower breast and back black. Central tail feathers long and black.

Female in winter has white head and neck with brown cap, brown patch below cheek, and dark grey beak. Breast and back brown. Flanks and undertail coverts white.

Surf Scoter

Macreuse à front blanc

Melanitta perspicillata

L 48–60 CM (19–23.5 IN) | **WS** 76–77 CM (30–30.5 IN)

A list of colourful duck noses would include the male Surf Scoter's brilliant white, orange, yellow, and black beak. This can be surprisingly hard to see at a distance, but the white head patches rule out other scoters. Female Surf Scoters can be tricky to separate from similar White-winged Scoters except when a flying or wing-stretching bird reveals the presence or absence of the White-winged's white speculum. (Surf Scoters' wings are all dark.) While Surf Scoters breed in the Hudson Bay Lowlands, away from most birders, they can be found in winter along the shore of Lake Ontario. The female makes a harsh quack.

Male has black head and body, white eye, and white patches on forehead and nape. Beak orange, yellow, and white with large black spot.

Female has brown head and body. Beak meets face in vertical line. Variable white patches on nape, base of beak, and cheek.

White-winged Scoter

Macreuse à ailes blanches

Melanitta deglandi

L 48-58 CM (19-23 IN) | **WS** 80 CM (31.5 IN)

The white wing patch known as the speculum is the best field mark for this duck, especially when it's viewed from a distance. However, the patch may be hidden while the bird is swimming. When foraging for submerged molluscs and crustaceans, scoters use their wings and feet to propel themselves to the bottom. Numbers of White-winged Scoters overwintering in the Great Lakes have increased because of a new food source: invasive zebra mussels. Since they were introduced, many diving ducks have added them to their diet and expanded their feeding ranges into new areas. May give a harsh quack.

Male has black head and body. White speculum sometimes visible while swimming (easy to see during flight). Small white crescent under white eye. Beak orange with black knob.

Female has brown head and body, dark eye, and whitish patches at base of beak and behind eye. Beak meets face in curved, not straight, line. White speculum sometimes visible while swimming.

Black Scoter

Macreuse à bec jaune

Melanitta americana

L 43–49 CM (17–19.5IN) | **WS** 70–72 CM (27.5–28.5 IN)

One of our least studied ducks, it wasn't until the last few decades that we started to understand where Black Scoters breed and moult in eastern North America. In Ontario, the first nesting record didn't come until 2006. Black Scoters are found in scattered locations along the Hudson Bay Lowlands during the breeding season. They often nest later than other waterfowl species; ducklings aren't seen until mid-July. During migration and winter, always search flocks of Surf and White-winged Scoters for Black Scoters. The all-black males and light-cheeked females usually are not hard to tell apart from the other two species. Female may make harsh growls.

Male all black with round head. Beak black with orange knob.

Female all brown. Cheeks light brown. Beak dark.

Bufflehead

Petit Garrot

Bucephala albeola

L 32-40 CM (12.5-16 IN) | **WS** 55 CM (21.5 IN)

This diving duck is so tiny that it can fit into the 6 cm (2.5 in) wide opening of an old Northern Flicker cavity nest. That's smaller than the diameter of a tennis ball. This allows Buffleheads to use nest cavities that are too small for larger cavity-nesting ducks, such as goldeneyes. This is important because female goldeneyes can kill female Buffleheads when they compete for larger nest sites. Female Buffleheads also compete for nest cavities with European Starlings. All this competition suggests how much we can help cavity-nesters when we put out nest boxes, increasing the number of nesting sites. Female may give a short croak.

Male has black head with colourful sheen if seen in good light, large white patch behind eye (but with no black border, as on Hooded Merganser), and grey beak.

Female all brown with lighter brown underparts, small white cheek patch, and grey beak. (In flight, note white in speculum.)

Common Goldeneye

Garrot à oeil d'or

Bucephala clangula

L 40–51 CM (16–20 IN) | **WS** 77–83 CM (30.5–32.5 IN)

The well-named goldeneye breeds in the boreal forest, where it lays its eggs in tree cavities. After the newly hatched ducklings jump from the nest, the female leads them to water. Sometimes, she abandons her ducklings to fend for themselves. In other cases, she may adopt other ducklings into her brood, a phenomenon called brood amalgamation or creching. If you see a female Common Goldeneye with a large number of ducklings, it is possible that they came from different broods, not just her own. The male's wings make a loud whistle in flight. Females can give a low growl.

Male has black head with green sheen and sloped forehead, black beak, and yellow eye. Circular white spot between eye and beak. Thin black lines between white flanks and black back. (In flight, watch for large white wing patches.)

Female has large brown head and yellow eye. Black beak has variable amounts of yellow (but rarely all yellow). Body greyish with white collar. (In flight, watch for white speculum and some white in shoulder.)

Barrow's Goldeneye

Garrot d'Islande

Bucephala islandica

L 43–48.5 CM (17–19 IN) | **WS** 70–73 CM (27.5–28.5 IN)

The Barrow's Goldeneye is an uncommon but regular visitor to Ontario. It is mostly a duck of western North America, but there is a small population in eastern North America, too. The time to find one is from late fall to spring, and the best place to look is just outside of Ottawa on the Ottawa River, though one may show up at other good waterfowl hot spots across southern Ontario west to the Saint Clair River. Your best strategy is to scan through flocks of floating ducks, looking carefully at every goldeneye you see and checking for the field marks of a Barrow's. The male's wings make a loud whistle in flight. Females can give a low growl.

Male has black head with purple (sometime greenish) sheen and steep forehead, black beak, and yellow eye. White crescent between eye and beak. White spots between white flanks and black back. (In flight, watch for large white wing patches crossed by black lines.)

Female has large dark brown head with yellow eye and mostly yellow beak. Body greyish with white collar. (In flight, watch for white speculum and some white in shoulder.

Ruddy Duck

Érismature rousse

Oxyura jamaicensis

L 35-43 CM (14-17 IN) | **WS** 56-62 CM (22-24.5 IN)

The courtship displays of many male ducks can be comical to watch, but the Ruddy Duck's Bubbling Display likely evokes the most smiles. First, the male raises his stiff tail straight up and erects two little horns on his head. Then he rapidly slaps his bright blue beak on his chest while pumping his head up and down, making bubbles on the water's surface. He finishes by sticking out his neck and making a ridiculous-sounding guttural whine. Unlike most other ducks, Ruddy Ducks form pairs on the breeding grounds, not at their wintering or migration sites. This means that if you find Ruddies in spring, you will have a good chance of seeing this wonderful performer in action. Females may make a nasal *aaaaaah*.

Male has black cap, white cheeks, and bright blue beak. Body reddish chestnut. Tail long and dark. (In flight, males and females have no markings on upper wings.)

Female has dark brown cap and light cheek divided by brown line. Body greyish brown. Tail long and dark.

Hooded Merganser

Harle couronné

Lophodytes cucullatus

L 40-49 CM (16-19.5 IN) | **WS** 60-66 CM (23.5-26 IN)

Our smallest merganser, the Hooded Merganser sometimes lays its eggs in the nests of Wood Ducks, Common Mergansers, and Common Goldeneyes—although, to be fair, these species have been known to lay eggs in Hooded Merganser nests, and in each other's nests, too. Spreading your eggs around is likely a response to predation: If your nest is predated, all of your eggs are eaten. But if you don't put all of your eggs in one basket, then some of them might survive in another duck's successful nest. Hooded Mergansers breed across most of the province, from its southern tip to 54°N in the Hudson Bay Lowlands. Females give a harsh croak, sometimes in a series when in flight.

Male's black breast, back and head marked with white. Thin beak and yellow eye. Long white crest bordered with black can be raised and lowered. Chestnut flanks. Tail long. (In flight, watch for large white wing patches)

Female has greyish-brown head and body and reddish-chestnut crest. Beak thin and black above and yellow below. (In flight, watch for white speculum.)

Common Merganser

Grand Harle

Mergus merganser

L 54–71 CM (21.5–28 IN) | **WS** 86 CM (34 IN)

The Common Merganser is found across the Northern Hemisphere. In Ontario, it is often associated with cottage country. Many people get to know it by watching females and their broods swim past their docks. The females may have had to lead their ducklings up to 2 km (1.2 mi) to the water, depending on where their cavity nests were. This is quite a feat because of their feet: they're placed farther back on their bodies than on other ducks, making walking difficult. Females give a harsh croak, sometimes in a series when in flight.

Male has green head, long, thin, red beak, and white neck, breast, and flanks. Back black. Feet reddish orange. (In flight, watch for large white wing patches.)

Female grey with long, thin, orange beak. Brown crested head contrasts sharply with white chin and neck. (In flight, watch for white speculum.)

Red-breasted Merganser

Harle huppé

Mergus serrator

L 51-64 CM (20-25 IN) | **WS** 66-74 CM (26-29 IN)

The Red-breasted Merganser looks similar to the Common Merganser, but the male Red-breasted is darker, with a chestnut breast, wide white collar, and punk rocker's crest. The two females are tougher to tell apart: look for the Red-breasted's less distinct whitish throat, thinner beak, and larger crest. Red-breasted Mergansers nest on the ground. This make their nests less secure than the cavity nests of Common Mergansers, but Red-breasteds are not restricted by available cavities and also have to lead their ducklings a shorter distance to water. Females give a harsh croak, sometimes in a series when in flight.

Male has green head with crest (sometimes split in two), long, thin, red beak, white collar, and reddish-brown breast. White panel divides black back from grey flanks. (In flight, watch for large white wing patches.)

Female has brown head with crest (sometimes split in two) and long, thin, orange beak. White throat blends into neck. Breast whitish and body grey. (In flight, watch for white speculum.)

Wild Turkey

Dindon sauvage
Meleagris gallopavo

L 110–115 CM (43.5–45.5 IN) | **WS** 125–144 CM (49–56.5 IN)

This species is both native and introduced. Wild Turkeys were wild in southern Ontario until 1909, when hunting and habitat loss finally extirpated them from the province. A reintroduction program that started in 1984 was wildly successful, and now this species has a wider distribution in Ontario than it did before it disappeared, and it is using more habitats. Wild Turkeys can now be seen along highways and roads in densely forested areas, such as Algonquin Provincial Park. Listen for, you guessed it, gobbling! The male produces a far-carrying, falling gobble. Females may give an emphatic cluck.

Male extremely large and dark brown but shiny. Head very small, warty, and blue and red. Tail feathers (spread during display) have dark bands and rufous tips. Female duller and smaller than male and has less colour on head.

Gray Partridge

Perdrix grise
Perdix perdix

L 30–33 CM (12–13 IN) | **WS** 53–56 CM (21–22 IN)

Six Gray Partridges were released near Brantford in 1909, and others were introduced in the next few decades in different parts of the province. In the first Ontario Breeding Bird Atlas (1981–85), the gamebird was found in 112 survey squares, but this declined to 68 squares in the second atlas (2001–05). In the first year of the third atlas (2021), it was found in only five squares, showing that not every introduced species is invasive and forever. Makes harsh rasping calls.

Male grey with rich buffy head, brownish back, thick chestnut bars on flanks, and dark belly patch. Tail short with chestnut outer tail feathers. (Female duller with no belly patch and paler face.)

Ruffed Grouse

Gélinotte huppée

Bonasa umbellus

L 40-50 CM (16-19.5 IN) | **WS** 50-64 CM (19.5-25 IN)

The male Ruffed Grouse makes a distinctive drumming sound that you can almost feel as well as hear. So low that you may miss it at first, it is thought to advertise the bird's presence to both females and other males. To make it, he beats the air with his wings so fast that they create a vacuum. After each beat, air rushes in, making a small sonic boom. It is not surprising that this species is sometimes called the "drummer."

Slender and brown or greyish above with small crested head, barred flanks, and long tail with thick black band near tip. Legs and feet feathered. Can be tame or wary.

Spruce Grouse

Tétras du Canada
Canachites canadensis

L 39–40.5 CM (15.5–16 IN) | **WS** 54.5–57.5 CM (21.5–22.5 IN)

Algonquin Provincial Park is one of the most accessible places to see the Spruce Grouse, a bird of the boreal forest. The species can be tough to find, but not always. Sometimes you can walk right past one that's hiding and not know it is there. Other times, the bird may seem oblivious to your presence and walk up to your feet. The Spruce Grouse eats pine, spruce, fir, and tamarack needles, which have very low nutritional value. The bird compensates by having a larger digestive system than other grouse species, allowing it to process more food. May make a series of low clucks. A displaying male may clap its wings above its back while flying.

Male has grey head with red eyebrow, black breast, and white triangles on belly and flanks. Tail black with buffy tip. Legs and feet feathered. Female (right) grey or brown with fine dark barring and white spots, especially on belly and flanks. May show indistinct whitish border on throat. Tail darkish with buffy tip.

Sharp-tailed Grouse

Tétras à queue fine

Tympanuchus phasianellus

L 38–48.5 CM (15–19 IN) | **WS** 62–65 CM (24.5–25.5 IN)

A western bird, the Sharp-tailed Grouse can be found across
northern Ontario, where it prefers open, grassy spaces with
scattered trees or islands of forest. Males display by dancing
with other males in an arena called a lek. Then females choose
which dancer will be their mate. The dances include foot
stomping and tail flicking and sounds that scientists know
as the Cork, the Chilk, the Gobble, and the Whine. The best
places to look for Sharp-tailed Grouse in Ontario include areas
around Sault Ste. Marie, Manitoulin Island, Rainy River, and
Cochrane and, for the adventurous, from the Polar Bear Express
on its way to Moosonee.

Chicken-like, with pointed pale tail.
Brownish above, whitish below, with small
crest and yellow eyebrow (may be hard
to see). Flight feathers brown, spotted
with white. Legs and feet feathered.

Ring-necked Pheasant

Faisan de Colchide

Phasianus colchicus

L 50–89 CM (19.5–35 IN) | **WS** 56–86 CM (22–34 IN)

The Ring-necked Pheasant is native to Asia and Europe and was introduced to North America in the 1800s for hunting purposes, but wild populations are now declining. Without additional releases of captive-bred individuals, it is thought that the species could die out in Ontario. Deep snow in certain winters and the maturing of open habitat are factors in its decline. Found along scrubby field edges, hedgerows, and scrubby areas around wetlands, pheasants are often heard more than they are seen; listen for a harsh, raspy double crow made by the male.

Male has dark head with red face, yellow beak, and white neck ring. Body chestnut and orange, with grey wings and rump and extremely long, pointed, orangish-brown tail with dark bars. Legs and feet bare.

Female buffy brown, lighter underneath with dark bars on upperparts. Tail long and pointed with dark bars.

Pied-billed Grebe

Grèbe à bec bigarré

Podilymbus podiceps

L 30–38 CM (12–15 IN) | **WS** 45–62 CM (17.5–24.5 IN)

This grebe catches many different food items, including cray-fish, insects, fish, even frogs and tadpoles, and like other grebe species, it is known to eat a lot of its own feathers. Studies have shown the contents of a Pied-billed Grebe's stomach might be more than 50 percent feathers. Adults may even feed feathers to their young right after they hatch. It is thought that swallowed feathers may stop sharp fish bones from entering the intestines from the stomach. The bones then either dissolve or are regurgitated in feather-filled pellets. The grebe's weird song is an echoing, hollow series of *cow* notes that ends with gulping noises interspersed with rasping inhalation sounds.

Summer adult has brownish-grey head and body, black throat, and dark forehead, as well as white eye ring and dark eye. Strong thick beak with black ring. Fluffy white tail.

Winter adult lacks black. Throat whitish. No or smudgy ring on pale beak.

Red-necked Grebe

Grèbe jougris

Podiceps grisegena

L 43–56 CM (17–22 IN) | **WS** 61–88 CM (24–34.5 IN)

This showy grebe can be found on the Great Lakes as well as the Niagara and other large rivers during migration and, when the water is open, even over the winter. But the best place to see it is Bronte Harbour in Oakville, where for over two decades at least one pair has nested, much to the delight of the locals and visiting birders. The whole community celebrates the hatching of the eggs and the antics of the little striped young. Sounds include a nasal grunting as well as wails, rattles, and whinnies.

Adult in summer has black cap, whitish cheek, and dark eye. Long sharp beak dark on top and yellow underneath. Neck long and reddish chestnut. Body brown.

Adult in winter brownish grey, with faint whitish patch behind eye and whitish throat and indistinct collar. May have reddish-chestnut wash on pale neck. Flanks whitish.

Horned Grebe

Grèbe esclavon

Podiceps auritus

L 31–38 CM (12–15 IN) | **WS** 44–46 CM (17.5–18 IN)

The Horned Grebe's North American breeding distribution is mostly western and central Canada. Northwestern Ontario is at the extreme eastern edge of this area, but during migration, and sometimes in winter, the grebe can be found at many Great Lakes shoreline locations in southern Ontario. Even when viewed from a distance, its short body and smallish head help distinguish it from Red-necked Grebes, Red-throated Loons, and ducks. May make a rough, high-pitched, gull-like cry as well as trills and chatters.

Adult in summer has large black head, thick golden tufts or "horns," red eye, and black pointed beak with light tip. Neck, breast, and flanks reddish chestnut. Back dark with lighter scaling.

Adult in winter has white head and neck with dark cap and nape, smudgy grey on sides of neck, red eye, and pale pointed beak with light tip. Red line between beak and eye. Flanks whitish and mottled.

Eared Grebe

Grèbe à cou noir

Podiceps nigricollis

L 30-35 CM (12-14 IN) | **WS** 52-55 CM (20.5-21.5 IN)

In winter, this mostly western species can be tricky to distinguish from a Horned Grebe. Watch for the Eared's thinner, darker neck, darker cheek, and thinner upturned beak. While the Eared Grebe is found in many places on the planet, it has bred in Ontario only in the Rainy River area in the northwestern part of the province and once near Thedford, in southern Ontario. While rare, it does show up annually during migration in southern Ontario, so scrutinize all Horned Grebes during spring and fall. Repeats a three-part whistle: *oooo-eee-a, oooo-eee-a, oooo-eee-a.*

Adult in winter has black head with white chin and indistinct collar. Head may be pointed on top. Beak pale, black on top and at tip, and slightly upturned. Neck mostly dark. Breast white, back dark, and flanks whitish and mottled.

Adult in summer has black head and neck, and thin yellow feathers radiate back from red eye. Head may show pointed crest. Beak thin, black, pointed, and slightly upturned. Back black with rufous wash on flanks and breast.

Rock Pigeon

Pigeon biset
Columba livia

L 30–36 CM (12–14 IN) | **WS** 50–67 CM (19.5–26.5 IN)

The Rock Pigeon is everywhere. It has been introduced to every continent on the planet except Antarctica, and it has existed in North America for 400 years. Most pigeons are the common grey "blue-bar" morph, but there are many other colour types, including brown, all white, and pied. Rock Pigeons can nest in Ontario at any time of the year. In Toronto, Canada's biggest city, the peak nesting period is between December and April. Because they are not restricted to a certain nesting season, pairs can successfully raise young up to four times in a calendar year. Gives a deep rolling coo.

Highly variable. Most have dark grey head with greenish and/or purplish sheen. Body and wings light grey with dark wing bars. Rump usually white. Tail grey with dark terminal band.

Mourning Dove

Tourterelle triste

Zenaida macroura

L 23-34 cm (9-13.5 in) | **WS** 45 cm (17.5 in)

Most of us are already familiar with this beautiful bird, since the Mourning Dove often nests close to human habitation, including in hanging flowerpots, door wreaths, and window boxes. It may nest many times a year due to its long nesting season, from March to early October. The species' name comes from the mournful notes in its song: *coo-AH-cooo-cooo-cooo-cooo*. Milder winters and the presence of bird feeders have likely helped expand the dove's winter range.

Brown with black spots on wings and lower back. Small head and beak. Tail long and pointed, with white tips on outer feathers. (Juvenile has light edging on body and wing feathers.)

Yellow-billed Cuckoo

Coulicou à bec jaune
Coccyzus americanus

L 26–30 CM (10–12 IN) | **WS** 38–43 CM (15–17 IN)

Unlike its better-known European cousins, the Yellow-billed Cuckoo does not lay its eggs in other birds' nests—for the most part. It builds its own nest and raises its own young, but it may also lay its eggs in the nests of other Yellow-billed Cuckoos or even Black-billed Cuckoos. And there are cases of Yellow-billed Cuckoos laying in the nests of other species as well, but this doesn't seem very common. The species' nesting activity is famous: The time from the start of incubation to fledging may be as little as 17 days, one of the shortest periods of any bird. Song is a series of sharp *cuk* notes ending with slower *cowlp* notes.

Brown upperparts and white underparts. Long slightly curved beak dark above and yellow below. Primary feathers rufous. Tail long and brown, with black outer feathers tipped with large white spots.

Black-billed Cuckoo

Coulicou à bec noir

Coccyzus erythropthalmus

L 28-31 CM (11-12 IN) | **WS** 34-40 CM (13-16 IN)

Outbreaks of the invasive non-native Spongy Moth have denuded entire forests of tree leaves. Luckily for us, the Black-billed Cuckoo is on duty. An unsung hero, it is one of the only bird species that regularly eat hairy caterpillars. The hairs stick in the lining of the cuckoo's stomach until they become so numerous that they hamper digestion. Then the bird regurgitates the whole stomach lining as a pellet, hair and all. Black-billed Cuckoos can be common breeders in an area one year and rarer the next, as they follow outbreaks of spongy moths and native Eastern Tent and Forest Tent Caterpillars and fall webworms. Their song is a series of mellow *cu-cu-cu* notes. Since they can sometimes sound like Yellow-billed Cuckoos, identification by song alone is tricky.

Brown upperparts and white underparts, with long, slightly curved, black beak and red eye ring. Tail long and brown, with grey outer feathers tipped with small white crescents.

Common Nighthawk

Engoulevent d'Amérique

Chordeiles minor

L 22–24 CM (8.5–9.5 IN) | **WS** 53–57 CM (21–22.5 IN)

Whenever you hear a nasal buzzing *peent!*, look up and see if you can find a Common Nighthawk on the hunt. Every sighting of this crepuscular aerialist is a blessing, because the species has declined markedly in Ontario since the 1970s. The Ontario Breeding Bird Atlas documented that the probability of observation in some areas of the province decreased 67 percent from the early 1980s to the early 2000s. To find one, search in open places, such as the Carden Alvar. You just might see and hear the male's flight display, which results in a low *boooom* at the bottom of an impressive dive.

In flight, note long, thin, pointed wings, forked tail, white or buffy throat, white line at base of primaries, and finely barred breast, belly, and wing linings. (White patch on tail of males only.)

Small head with tiny beak that hides cavernous mouth. Throat patch white or buffy. Primary feathers long and dark. May sit with eyes closed, resembling bark-covered lump on branch or ground.

Eastern Whip-poor-will

Engoulevent bois-pourri

Antrostomus vociferus

L 22-26 CM (8.5-10 IN) | **WS** 45-48 CM (17.5-19 IN)

Listening to singing Eastern Whip-poor-wills has long been a favourite activity of cottagers across Ontario. Unfortunately, the experience isn't as common as it used to be. Like other birds that eat flying insects, the Eastern Whip-poor-will has declined alarmingly in the last several decades. Two of best places to hear one are along the edges of Georgian Bay and in the Carden Alvar. Research in Ontario revealed that the bird may time its nesting so its eggs hatch on average 10 days before the full moon. Since adults can hunt longer and catch more insects during moonlit nights, this means more food for fast-growing nestlings. Song is distinctive: *whip-poor-will*!

Large head with tiny beak that hides cavernous mouth. White or buffy throat hard to see when perched. May sit with eyes closed, resembling bark-covered lump on branch or ground. (In flight, note rounded wing tips and white or buffy corners on tail.)

Chimney Swift

Martinet ramoneur

Chaetura pelagica

L 12–15 CM (4.5–6 IN) | **WS** 27–30 CM (10.5–12 IN)

Here is a declining species that city folk can help. SwiftWatch is a Birds Canada/Oiseaux Canada project in which volunteer bird watchers monitor chimneys to assess the presence and abundance of Chimney Swifts. The birds often use old chimneys as their roosting and/or nesting sites. As the swifts dive into them in the evening, the monitors count the birds and report the totals to SwiftWatch. Chimney Swifts make a distinctive chatter of high-pitched and harsh chirps, repeated quickly.

Often described as flying cigar. Dark grey with short tail and beak and long wings held rigid. Flight stiffer and less graceful than swallows. Sometimes holds wings in V during courtship display flights.

Ruby-throated Hummingbird

Colibri à gorge rubis

Archilochus colubris

L 7-9 CM (3-3.5 IN) | **WS** 8-11 CM (3-4.5 IN)

All birds are marvelous, but the Ruby-throated Hummingbird, the only regularly occurring hummer in Ontario, is astonishing. It can fly forwards, backwards, and sideways and beat its wings over 50 times per second; it lays eggs the size of a blueberry; and it captures the heart of all who put out a nectar feeder. To attract one, fill a feeder with nectar made from the preferred ratio of four parts water to one part plain white sugar. Having a feeder close by will allow you to get an up-close look at the aerial prowess of Ontario's smallest bird. Besides the hum of its wings, the Ruby-throated Hummingbird also makes a chattering call.

Male tiny, with long thin beak, black mask, and white spot behind eye. Upperparts iridescent green, underparts white with greenish flanks. Brilliant iridescent red throat can look black depending on light angle. Tail black and forked.

Female similar but lacks red throat and black mask. Upperparts more golden green, flanks buffier, and tail shorter, with white tip. First-fall male similar but with a few red spots on throat.

Common Gallinule

Gallinule d'Amérique

Gallinula galeata

L 32–35 CM (12.5–14 IN) | **WS** 54–62 CM (21.5–24.5 IN)

Possessing a yellow-tipped beak, red frontal shield, and white side stripe, the Common Gallinule is not hard to identify—if you can see it. It's not particularly shy, as many rail species are, but because it lives in dense marshy areas, it can still be hard to find. Common Gallinules can also be rather noisy, but some of their calls are so similar to those of the American Coot that wildlife biologists sometimes record birds as "coot/gallinule" if they are only heard and not seen. Calls include whinnies, grunts, clucks, and honks. Common Gallinules breed in suitable marshes across southern Ontario.

Adult has black head, neck, and breast, pointed red beak with shield on forehead, and yellow beak tip. Body dark grey with white stripe on flank. White patch on side of tail. Legs yellow with long toes.

American Coot

Foulque d'Amérique

Fulica americana

L 39.5–43 CM (15.5–17 IN) | **WS** 58.5–63.5 CM (23–25 IN)

The American Coot could easily be voted bird with the coolest
toes. Its toes are lobed along their length, making the water-
bird look like it has Christmas cactuses on the ends of its legs.
The lobes allow for good propulsion while swimming and are
fine for walking, and, as a bonus, they help distribute the bird's
body weight, allowing it not to sink when it walks on soft
mud and floating plants. American Coots breed in deep-water
marshes across southern Ontario and at scattered locations in
northwestern Ontario and even up to James Bay. Calls include
whinnies, clucks, grunts, and honks.

Adult has black head, reddish eye, pointed
white beak with dark ring near tip, and
reddish and white shield on forehead.
Body dark grey with small white patch on
side of tail. Legs greenish with lobed toes.

Virginia Rail

Râle de Virginie

Rallus limicola

L 20-27 CM (8-10.5 IN) | **WS** 32-38 CM (12.5-15 IN)

While you might think that "skinny as a rail" describes someone who is as thin as a bar or rod, it could just as easily refer to someone who is as thin as a Virginia Rail. The bird is laterally flattened, as if someone picked it up by its sides and pressed inwards. The resulting shape allows it to move easily through cattails and other upright aquatic plants but makes seeing the rail very challenging. You are probably better off trying to listen for one calling from the depths of a wetland. It makes a variety of calls. Two of the most common are a grunting and accelerating *woink woink woink woink* and a sharper *kidick kidick kidick kidick kidick*.

Small and chicken-like, with long, drooping, orange beak and grey cheek. Back brown and streaked. Breast orangish brown. Flanks black and white streaked.

Sora

Marouette de Caroline

Porzana carolina

L 19-30 CM (7.5-12 IN) | **WS** 35-40 CM (13.5-15.5 IN)

Like the Virginia Rail, the Sora can be extremely hard to see. It lives in wetland areas densely packed with cattails, sedges, or bulrushes. The larger Virginia Rail also uses this habitat, but that doesn't stop the feisty Sora from defending its territory. Moreover, Soras eat more vegetable matter than Virginia Rails, so there may not be much competition for food. Soras make a distinctive rolling high whinny that descends in pitch and decelerates in speed.

Small and chicken-like, with short yellow beak, black mask, and grey face, throat, and breast. Upperparts brown with white markings and dark and white-streaked flanks.

Yellow Rail

Râle jaune

Coturnicops noveboracensis

L 13–18 cm (5–7 in) | **WS** 28–32 cm (11–12.5 in)

This rail's call could be the easiest to imitate of all Ontario birds. All you need to do is knock two small stones together in a repeated series of tick-tick, tick-tick-tick. But that is the only easy thing about the Yellow Rail, because finding one is very difficult. It breeds in wet sedge meadows from the Hudson Bay Lowlands to southern Ontario, but in extremely scattered locations. An early spring visit to the Carden Alvar may produce a calling migrant.

Small and chicken-like, with short yellow beak and whitish throat. Buffy and dark streaks with small white spots overall.

Sandhill Crane

Grue du Canada

Antigone canadensis

L 120 CM (47 IN) | **WS** 200 CM (78.5 IN)

The sound of the stately Sandhill Crane is impressive and distinctive, and a noisy flock flying overhead is a delight for the ears. The bird's echoing rattle call can be heard up to 4 km (2.5 mi) away. And more and more people can experience it, since crane populations are increasing in the breeding and migratory seasons, and the birds may overwinter in Ontario, too. The Long Point area, for example, may have thousands of overwintering Sandhill Cranes. It's definitely worth putting on some long underwear and warm socks to see them.

Tall and grey with rusty wash, long neck, and long dark legs. Face white with red forehead and long dark beak. In flight, extends neck, and legs usually trail behind. (Sometimes tucks legs up to body.)

Black-necked Stilt

Échasse d'Amérique

Himantopus mexicanus

L 35-39 CM (14-15.5 IN) | **WS** 71.5-75.5 CM (28-29.5 IN)

Before 2004, there had been only 13 sight records of Black-necked Stilt in Ontario. Then a pair nested near the Jarvis sewage lagoons. The tall and thin shorebird nests across a wide but patchy area of North America, including in Florida, along the east coast of the United States, in central and Pacific states, and sometimes in Alberta and Saskatchewan. The Jarvis record was Canada's easternmost, and stilts also raised young at the Strathroy sewage lagoons in 2022. It is thought that the bird may breed in southern Ontario more frequently in the future because of droughts in its regular breeding range and the effects of warmer summers due to climate change.

Tall, with long, thin, straight beak and very long reddish-pink legs. Adult male has black upperparts, white patch above eye, and white underparts. (Female has dark brown back.)

American Avocet

Avocette d'Amérique

Recurvirostra americana

L 43–47 CM (17–18.5 IN) | **WS** 72 CM (28.5 IN)

Unfortunately for Ontarians, the breeding range of this eye-popping shorebird lies in the central prairie and western regions of North America, although it has bred at the Sable Islands Provincial Nature Reserve in the Rainy River area. Birders in southwestern Ontario get a thrill when a flock shows up during migration at a shorebird hot spot such as Hillman Marsh Conservation Area. American Avocets have upturned beaks that they skim back and forth along the surface of the water to catch tiny invertebrate prey.

Large, with long, very thin, upturned, black beak and bluish-grey legs. Breeding adult has pale orange head and neck, white underparts, and black upperparts with thick white stripe through wing. (Winter avocet has grey head and neck. Juvenile in fall may have wash of orange on nape and head.)

Black-bellied Plover

Pluvier argenté

Pluvialis squatarola

L 28–29 cm (11–11.5 in) | **WS** 59–60 cm (23–23.5 in)

This large plover breeds in Canada's far north, winters as far south as the coastlines of central South America, and comes to Ontario only during spring and fall migration. It is seen on sod farms, on the shores of sewage lagoons, or in freshly plowed or flooded farmer's fields. Black-bellied Plovers often occur in great flocks and fly in large V's overhead. They're quite wary and may fly off at any sign of danger, taking other nearby shorebirds with them. Their call is a drawn-out whistled *peee-oooo-eeeee*.

Large plover. Breeding bird has black face, breast, and belly and white undertail coverts. Fairly heavy beak for a plover. White border around face, forehead, and sides of breast. Back dark and covered with white spots. Legs black.

Non-breeding bird greyish brown above with light spots and whitish below. Head larger, beak heavier, and eyebrow less distinct than on winter American Golden-Plover.

American Golden-Plover

Pluvier bronzé

Pluvialis dominica

L 24-28 CM (9.5-11 IN) | **WS** 65-67 CM (25.5-26.5 IN)

Smaller than the Black-bellied, the American Golden-Plover is another migrant through the province, although a few hundred pairs breed in the Hudson Bay Lowlands. The bulk of the population nests across Nunavut, the Northwest Territories, Yukon, and Alaska. During spring migration in May, scan through flocks of Black-bellied Plovers standing in farmer's fields north of Point Pelee National Park or at Hillman Marsh Conservation Area; American Golden-Plovers may be mixed in. Flight call is a repeated, two-part, sharp *ka-lick*.

Large plover. Breeding bird has black face, breast, belly, and undertail coverts and white border around face, forehead, and sides of breast. Upperparts dark with golden spots. Legs dark.

Non-breeding bird brown above and buffy below, with fairly distinct eyebrow. Beak and head smaller and eyebrow more distinct than non-breeding Black-bellied Plover.

Semipalmated Plover

Pluvier semipalmé

Charadrius semipalmatus

L 17-19 CM (6.5-7.5 IN) | **WS** 47-50 CM (18.5-19.5 IN)

The foraging technique of these plump little shorebirds always entertains observers. Looking like miniature Killdeer (but with only one breast band), Semipalmated Plovers run, stop, peck… run, stop, peck. They breed in the Hudson Bay Lowlands but, luckily for us, are commonly seen during migration farther south. Watch for them along Great Lakes beaches, mudflats, and flooded farm fields from May to early June on their way north and from mid-July to early October on their way south. Call is a low *chew-wee!*

Small plover. Breeding bird has dark brown back and white underparts. Forehead and cheek black with small white patch near beak. Beak orange with black tip. Collar black. Legs orange.

Non-breeding bird similar, but brown replaces black markings. Legs and beak duller.

Piping Plover

Pluvier siffleur

Charadrius melodus

L 15–19 CM (6–7.5 IN) | **WS** 35–41 CM (14–16 IN)

That this little plover likes the same beaches we do has caused controversy in the past but has also made it one of our most beloved birds. By 1977, it no longer nested on Ontario's Great Lakes beaches and was listed as Endangered, but in 2007 it started breeding here once again. Volunteer monitors, key players in a heartwarming wildlife success story, protect each pair and their eggs and young every day from April to August. The plover's call is a soft but clear whistled *pee-you*.

Small plover. Breeding bird has light sandy brown back, white underparts, white forehead with black line on top, broken black breast band, orange beak with black tip, and yellowish-orange legs.

Non-breeding bird similar but lacks black markings. Beak dark.

Killdeer

Pluvier kildir

Charadrius vociferus

L 20-28 CM (8-11 IN) | **WS** 46-48 CM (18-19 IN)

To protect its eggs and young, the avian thespian known as the Killdeer pretends to have a broken wing, leading foxes, raccoons, and other predators and curious children far from its nest. Then it takes flight, loudly calling *kill-deer*. The plover is our best-known shorebird because it is commonly seen in abandoned suburban properties, in large gravel parking lots, on flat rooftops, in farm fields, and along open shorelines, but its population has been declining for decades for unknown reasons.

Large and long tailed, with white forehead with dark stripes and red eye ring. Upperparts brown, underparts white. Two breast bands. Legs pale.

Performing distraction display, shows orange in tail feathers and rump (also seen in flight).

Whimbrel

Courlis corlieu

Numenius phaeopus

L 43–46 CM (17–18 IN) | **WS** 80–83 CM (31.5–32.5 IN)

Whimbrels are big shorebirds with a drooping beak, and they are eagerly anticipated by Ontario birders every May. During the bird's annual migration to the Hudson Bay Lowlands, there is even a Whimbrel Watch, a program started by the Toronto Ornithological Club, which counts the birds as they migrate past Colonel Samuel Smith Park along the shore of Lake Ontario. Morning is the best time to visit, because many Whimbrels leave the Atlantic coast of the United States the evening before, fly all night, and pass the park early in the day. Flight call is a fast, rolling, liquid trill.

Large and brown above and whitish or buffy below with long drooping beak. Head buffy with dark lateral crown stripes and dark eye lines. Primaries dark. Legs grey.

Hudsonian Godwit

Barge hudsonienne
Limosa haemastica

L 37–42 CM (14–17 IN) | **WS** 69–74 CM (27–29 IN)

Both of Ontario's godwit species are uncommon migrants
in southern parts of the province, so finding one is always a
treat. Not surprisingly given its name, the Hudsonian Godwit
breeds in the Hudson Bay Lowlands. Try to see one during fall
migration at a shorebird hot spot such as Windermere Basin
in Hamilton. This godwit was once known as the "ring-tailed
marlin" because of the band on its tail and because its long
slender beak is reminiscent of the pointy-nosed fish called the
marlin. Call is a loud *kee-wee*.

Very large shorebird. Breeding bird has long,
upcurved, orange beak with black tip. Face
pale with dark eye line. Breast and belly
mottled rufous. In flight, note white stripe in
wing, white rump, and dark tip to tail. Wing
lining black. Non-breeding godwit plain
greyish brown with whitish underparts.
Eyebrow whitish. Eye line dark.

Marbled Godwit

Barge marbrée

Limosa fedoa

L 42–48 CM (16–19 IN) | **WS** 70–81 CM (27–32 IN)

This mostly western species is usually seen in the province during migration, as most Marbled Godwits breed in the prairies. In Ontario, they breed in the southern part of the province's northwest as well as along the shores of James Bay in the far north. Godwits use their long beaks to probe for invertebrates in mudflats. The beak's tip is flexible, allowing the bird to grab hold of its meal, an important adaptation since the bird can't open its whole beak when it is stuck in the mud. Call is a repeated *kaa-waa*.

Note buffy patch in wing, buffy-cinnamon wing lining, and buffy tail with dark barring.

Very large, with long, upcurved, pinkish beak with black tip and pale face with dark eye line. Upperparts speckled brown and buffy with fine breast barring. Non-breeding bird has less barring on breast.

Ruddy Turnstone

Tournepierre à collier

Arenaria interpres

L 16–21 CM (6–8 IN) | **WS** 50–57 CM (20–22 IN)

Beaks are great indicators of how birds forage. The Ruddy Turnstone, as its name implies, uses its stout beak to flip over stones, shells, and washed-up aquatic plants while searching for invertebrate prey. The turnstone can also use its beak to pry open mussels, search cracks in shoreline rocks, and dig in sandy beaches. In breeding plumage, it is one of our most colourful shorebirds. We get to see it only during migration. It breeds on Arctic islands, far to the north. Call is a loud *kew*.

Breeding bird rufous, black, and white. Beak triangular and pointed. Legs short and red.

Non-breeding bird exchanges much rufous, black, and white with brown but still has dark patches on breast. Legs orangish.

Red Knot

Bécasseau maubèche

Calidris canutus

L 23-27 CM (9-11 IN) | **WS** 57-60 CM (22-24 IN)

Numbers of this beautiful shorebird have dropped precipitously since the early 1980s, leading the subspecies *rufa* to be listed as Endangered in Canada in 2007. Each year, it completes an arduous circuit from the Canadian High Arctic to Tierra del Fuego, Chile, at the southern tip of South America, and back. The Hudson Bay Lowlands and other stopovers provide crucial resting and refueling spots along the way. The knots arrive in spring at one of them, Delaware Bay, after flying as many as seven days non-stop. Then they double their body weight, eating horseshoe crab eggs. The food is so important that local overfishing of horseshoe crabs is the likely cause of the bird's demise. The Red Knot's plight shows that breeding, wintering, and migration areas are all important. Nations need to work together to save our world's birds.

Non-breeding bird mostly grey above and white below with white eyebrow and some grey barring on flanks. Legs dark to yellowish. Juvenile (shown here) has light edges on back and wing feathers. Breeding bird mostly rufous, especially on head, breast, and belly, with medium-length dark beak. Undertail coverts white with dark spots. Legs dark.

Stilt Sandpiper

Bécasseau à échasses

Calidris himantopus

L 20-23 CM (8-9 IN) | **WS** 38-41 CM (15-16 IN)

The Stilt Sandpiper can sometimes go unnoticed in a mixed flock of shorebirds. Its legs aren't unusually long or really short. Its beak isn't an overly strange shape or size. Plus, it isn't common during migration in southern Ontario, so birders don't get much of a chance to get to know it. Watch for the chestnut patch on its cheeks (especially in breeding plumage), its yellowish-green legs, and longish slightly drooping beak. In Ontario, Stilt Sandpipers nest in the Hudson Bay Lowlands. Call is a quiet *tew*.

Tallish, with long drooping beak. Breeding bird has chestnut cheek patch, light eyebrow, and darkish eye line. Upperparts brown with light spots. Underparts whitish with dark barring. Legs longish and yellowish green. Non-breeding bird greyish with white underparts, light eyebrow, and dark eye line. May show bit of chestnut cheek patch.

Pectoral Sandpiper

Bécasseau à poitrine cendrée

Calidris melanotos

L 20–24 CM (8–10 IN) | **WS** 44–46 CM (17–18 IN)

Named for its patterned breast, the Pectoral Sandpiper is known to have bred only once in Ontario. Two flightless young were found in 1948 in the Hudson Bay Lowlands, the most southerly confirmed breeding record for the species. The sandpiper is a common migrant through Ontario in both spring and fall and can be observed in large flocks in wet agricultural fields and open wet expanses along rivers, lakes, and marshes. It makes a series of short, rough trills.

Brown with white spots and rufous edging on upperparts. Slightly drooping beak light at base. Underparts white. Breast buffy with dark streaks. Legs yellow.

Purple Sandpiper

Bécasseau violet

Calidris maritima

L 20–22 cm (8–9 in) | **WS** 42–46 cm (16–18 in)

Like the Red-bellied Woodpecker and Ring-necked Duck, this bird was likely named by an early naturalist holding a specimen. If you look carefully, you might be able to see a slight purplish sheen on its back and wing feathers. The Purple Sandpiper generally winters on the east coast of North America, but it can be found in small numbers in southern Ontario from late fall to mid-winter. The best places to look include the Niagara River just above the falls, the Erieau pier, and various locations along the west end of Lake Ontario. May give quiet but harsh chattering calls while feeding.

Plump. Non-breeding sandpiper grey above and white below with longish beak with light base and indistinct eye ring. Legs yellow. (Juvenile browner; some feathers with white edges.)

Sanderling

Bécasseau sanderling

Calidris alba

L 18-20 CM (7-8 IN) | **WS** 35-36 CM (14-15 IN)

These might be the most enjoyable sandpipers to watch. Foraging along a Great Lakes shore, they skitter toward the water as one wave recedes, only to turn around and skitter back up the beach as the next wave comes in, their legs a blur of motion. Sanderlings breed in the High Arctic. Watch for them during spring and fall migrations as they travel to and from the east coast, where they overwinter. Call is a chattery series of short *chit* notes.

Non-breeding bird pale, grey above and white below, with whitish face and dark area at bend of wing. Beak and legs dark. When wings are folded, wing tips extend just past end of tail. (In flight, long white wing stripe contrasts with dark wing.)

Breeding bird mottled rufous. Underparts white.

Dunlin
Bécasseau variable
Calidris alpina

L 16-22 CM (6-9 IN) | **WS** 36-38 CM (14-15 IN)

In breeding plumage, the black belly patch on this little sandpiper is easy to see both when it's foraging and when it flies by in big speedy flocks. And Dunlin need to be speedy, because their main predators are Peregrine Falcons and Merlins. By staying in tight flocks and coordinating their quick dips and turns, they are less vulnerable than when they fly on their own. Dunlin breed in the coastal tundra of the Hudson Bay Lowlands and across the southern Arctic to the coasts of Alaska. Call is harsh *jeet*.

Breeding bird has bright rufous upperparts, greyish head, and long drooping beak. Black belly patch distinctive. Legs dark.

Non-breeding bird light grey above and white below, with whitish eyebrow and indistinct eye line. Lacks black belly patch, so note long drooping beak.

Western Sandpiper

Bécasseau d'Alaska

Calidris mauri

L 14–17 CM (5–7 IN) | **WS** 35–37 CM (14–15 IN)

Five little sandpipers, often referred to as peeps, can be tricky to identify: the Western, Least, Semipalmated, Baird's, and White-rumped. Not surprisingly, based on its name, the Western is much more common in western North America, but it can still show up in Ontario during migration. When one is in a group of other peeps, notice its slightly droopier beak, almost like a little Dunlin. Also, Western Sandpipers may stand a little more upright than other peeps or look a bit off balance, because their legs seem to be placed farther back on the body than on the Semipalmated. Call is a high, short *chit*.

Non-breeding bird brownish grey above and white below. Some streaking on breast.

Tiny. Breeding bird has some bright rufous on crown, cheeks, and back, slightly drooping beak, and streaks on breast. When wings are folded, wing tips extend to tail tip.

Least Sandpiper

Bécasseau minuscule

Calidris minutilla

L 13–15 CM (5–6 IN) | **WS** 27–28 CM (10.5–11 IN)

Weighing as much as a Song Sparrow, the Least Sandpiper is North America's smallest sandpiper, although Semipalmated and Western Sandpipers are pretty close in size. Luckily for us, the Least is the only peep with yellowish legs, but take care: the legs of a Least Sandpiper that has been foraging in mud can look just as dark as the legs of other peeps. Call is a short high-pitched trill.

Tiny. Non-breeding sandpiper brownish above and white below with a few streaks on breast and slight droop at end of beak. Legs yellowish. When wings are folded, wing tips project to tail tip.

Juvenile (fall) with white spots on wings and back and rufous feather edges. Breast markings usually restricted to sides. (Breeding bird similar but with more streaking on breast and less rufous.)

Semipalmated Sandpiper

Bécasseau semipalmé

Calidris pusilla

L 15–18 cm (6–7 in) | **WS** 35–37 cm (14–14.5 in)

The Semipalmated Sandpiper is one of our more commonly seen peeps. Studying it will help you recognize other small sandpipers. Often identified by what it doesn't have, the sandpiper has no white rump, no yellow legs, and no drooping beak, and when its wings are folded, the wing tips do not extend past the tail. In 2012 it was estimated that there were over two million Semipalmated Sandpipers, making it one of the most populous North American shorebirds, even though these numbers represent a significant drop from the 3.5 million birds estimated in the 1990s. Semipalmateds breed on the tundra in the Hudson Bay Lowlands. Call is a loud *chup* or fast series of *tee* notes.

Juvenile has light edges on wing and back feathers. Some buff on breast.

Tiny. Breeding bird brownish above and white below and often less rufous than other peeps, with streaks on breast. Beak mostly straight and dark. Legs dark. When wings are folded, wing tips project to tail tip.

White-rumped Sandpiper

Bécasseau à croupion blanc

Calidris fuscicollis

L 15-18 CM (6-7 IN) | **WS** 40-44 CM (16-17 IN)

The White-rumped and Baird's Sandpipers are bigger than the other three peeps. They also have longer wings; when their wings are folded, the tips extend beyond the end of the tail. (This is one of the first things you should look for on any peep.) Shape differences separate White-rumped from Baird's, but the best field mark, not surprisingly, is the White-rumped's white rump, which becomes visible when the bird flies or stretches and is unique among Ontario's small sandpipers. White-rumped Sandpipers nest in the High Arctic, so they are seen in the province only during migration. Call is a high-pitched squeak.

Small. Non-breeding sandpiper brownish grey above and white below, with some markings on breast. Legs dark. When wings are folded, wing tips project past tail tip. May show light orange on base of beak. (In flight, watch for fully white rump.)

Breeding bird has white and rufous markings on back and wings. Faintly streaked breast.

Baird's Sandpiper

Bécasseau de Baird

Calidris bairdii

L 14–18 cm (5–7 in) | **WS** 35–38 cm (14–15 in)

The Baird's Sandpiper, the other "long-winged peep," is observed in Ontario less commonly than the White-rumped because much of its migration goes through the center of the continent, especially in spring. Most individuals seen are juveniles in fall. While you can't count on it completely, habitat can also be a clue to identification: a Baird's Sandpiper is much more likely than a White-rumped to show up in a sod field or short grass area. And it should be noted that both sandpipers have longer wings for a reason: they fly farther south than the other peeps, some making it to the southern tip of South America. Call of the Baird's Sandpiper is a harsh and high-pitched *keer*.

Small. Non-breeding sandpiper brown above and white below. Legs dark. When wings are folded, wing tips extend past tail tip.

Breeding bird has some white markings and dark spots on back and wings. Juvenile has distinct light edges on back and wing feathers. Buff on breast.)

Buff-breasted Sandpiper

Bécasseau roussâtre
Calidris subruficollis

L 19–23 CM (7–9 IN) | **WS** 43–46 CM (16–18 IN)

The Buff-breasted Sandpiper is one of the most sought-after birds on the Ontario list. It is a rare migrant and most likely to be found in fall. It likes open areas, such as sod farms and flooded fields, but can be found on shorelines and at sewage lagoons as well. Some of the best places to search for one from late August to mid-September are Presqu'ile Provincial Park, the fields just north of Point Pelee National Park, and the sod farms and wet fields around Beeton. Buff-breasted populations have been decreasing since the late 1800s, when commercial hunting was allowed. More recently, habitat loss and pesticide use on migration and at overwintering sites have harmed overall numbers.

Face and underparts buffy. Head squarish with short dark beak. Back dark. Legs yellow. Often holds itself more upright than most other sandpipers.

Upland Sandpiper

Maubèche des champs

Bartramia longicauda

L 28–32 CM (11–13 IN) | **WS** 47–66 CM (18–26 IN)

Wheeet! Wheeeeooooooooooo! That's the wolf whistle of the Upland Sandpiper, one of the few sandpipers that breed in southern Ontario. It prefers open grasslands with exposed perches, so you are likely to see one standing on an old wooden fence post or abandoned survey stake. Like populations of other grassland bird species, Upland Sandpiper numbers are dwindling in Ontario. In the Carolinian region, the probability of seeing one during the breeding season dropped by 52 percent from the early 1980s to the early 2000s. The Carden Alvar is still a great place to see them during the breeding season.

Smallish and squarish head on long neck, with yellowish beak with black tip. Mottled upperparts, barred underparts, and long tail. Legs yellow. Stands more upright than most sandpipers.

Short-billed Dowitcher

Bécassin roux

Limnodromus griseus

L 23–32 CM (9–12 IN) | **WS** 46–56 CM (18–22 IN)

Dowitchers are chunky shorebirds with long beaks. They feed along shorelines, moving their heads up and down like a sewing machine needle. Often in large flocks, dowitchers have a great in-flight field mark: a long, white back patch. (See Long-billed Dowitcher photo.) The Short-billed Dowitcher is the more common of Ontario's two dowitcher species. It is also the only one to breed in the province (in the Hudson Bay Lowlands and northern parts of the boreal forest). Call is a whistled *tu-tu-tu*, often given when it takes off.

Breeding bird buffy rufous with mottled back, light eyebrow, dark eye line, and long straight beak. Spots on neck and sides of breast, bars on flanks. Belly whitish. (Long white back patch seen in flight.)

Juvenile plainer, especially on underparts. (Non-breeding adult greyer.)

Long-billed Dowitcher

Bécassin à long bec

Limnodromus scolopaceus

L 28–30 CM (11–12 IN) | **WS** 46–49 CM (18–19 IN)

Long-billed and Short-billed Dowitchers are tough to tell apart. You'd think that you could use bill length for help, but that feature is difficult to see in the field and females have longer beaks than males. In spring, Long-billeds have more dark spotting on the sides of their necks than Short-billeds, and in late summer and fall, the Long-billed Dowitcher's migration window is later than the Short-billed's. The time periods overlap, but any dowitcher in southern Ontario past mid-September is likely a juvenile of the rarer Long-billed. Long-billeds also make a higher and sharper *keek*. (Compare to the Short-billed's lower and more fluid *tu-tu-tu*.)

Plumper and rounder-bodied than Short-billed. Breeding bird buffy rufous with mottled back, light eyebrow, dark eye line, and long straight beak. Bars on neck and sides of breast. Dark and white bars on flanks. Belly rufous. (Juvenile plainer and greyer.) In flight, both dowitcher species show distinctive white back patch.

American Woodcock

Bécasse d'Amérique

Scolopax minor

L 25–31 CM (10–12 IN) | **WS** 42–48 CM (16–19 IN)

This incredible shorebird is about as un-shorebird-like as you can get. Instead of hanging out along a shore, it frequents wet woods, swamp edges, and damp scrub, and its displays are spectacular. Just as it is getting dark, the male moves to an open area called a lek and flies into the darkening sky, spiralling upwards in wide circles while making a unique twitter sound with specialized primary feathers. Then, before it disappears into the heavens, it plummets back to earth, zigzagging while chirping. When it finally lands, you will hear its call, a buzzy, nasal *peent!* A local nature club may have a woodcock walk for you to attend on an evening in April or May.

Round body with well-camouflaged upperparts and buffy underparts, large eyes on top of domed head, long pale beak, and short neck. Tail and legs short.

Wilson's Snipe

Bécassine de Wilson

Gallinago delicata

L 27–32 CM (10–13 IN) | **WS** 41–44 CM (16–17 IN)

Though not as awe-inspiring as the antics of the American Wood-cock, the winnowing of the Wilson's Snipe is plenty entertaining. The evening display is performed mostly by males. The bird flies upwards in a wide circle, then dives vertically, using its outer tail feathers to make a spooky, wavering, hollow sound. Then it flies up again and repeats the process. One bird was recorded doing this for over an hour. Wilson's Snipes prefer scrubby swamps, fens, bogs, and vegetated edges of rivers and ponds.

Round body with pale face with dark lateral crown stripes and eye line and very long beak. Light stripes on back and mottled spots on breast. Bars on flanks. Short yellowish legs.

Spotted Sandpiper

Chevalier grivelé

Actitis macularius

L 18–20 CM (7–8 IN) | **WS** 37–40 CM (14–16 IN)

Not only is the Spotted Sandpiper likely our most commonly seen sandpiper, but it is also one of the easiest to identify. Its spotted breast and belly, combined with an orange beak and legs, are distinctive. As well, it flies with stiff wings, and it bobs its tail as it forages, making it even more obvious what it is. Female Spotted Sandpipers can have more than one mate, and the males provide most or all of the care for the young, though some pairs share the parental duties. Call is a loud *teet-teet-teet*.

Breeding bird has brown upperparts, white underparts, white eyebrow, and orange beak and legs, as well as spots on breast and belly. Bobs rear end.

Juvenile has finely barred upperparts, plain white breast with some brown on sides of breast, and yellowish legs. (Non-breeding adult similar but lacks fine barring.)

Solitary Sandpiper

Chevalier solitaire

Tringa solitaria

L 19–23 CM (7–9 IN) | **WS** 41–43 CM (16–17 IN)

Since shorebirds are usually observed at the edges of puddles in open fields or along beaches, it is fun to see the Solitary Sandpiper grabbing insect larvae from a forested ephemeral pond during spring migration. The shorebird likes trees in another way, too: it nests in them. Our only sandpiper to do so, it uses the old nests of other birds. Unfortunately, you are not likely to see its nest since it breeds in the boreal forest and Hudson Bay Lowlands. Also, up to 2005, only five nests had been found in Ontario, even though birds have been seen with fledglings in many northern Ontario locations. Call is a high *pee-weet* or *pee-wee-weet*.

Adult breeding bird brown above and white below, with distinct white "spectacles," white spots on upperparts, and fine streaks on sides of breast. White outer tail feathers have thick dark bands. Legs greenish yellow.

Non-breeding sandpiper similar but with less spotting above. Smudgy brown on breast. (Juvenile has more spotting above than non-breeding adult.)

Lesser Yellowlegs

Petit Chevalier

Tringa flavipes

L 23-25 cm (9-10 in) | **WS** 59-64 cm (23-25 in)

The long yellow legs of the Lesser Yellowlegs are a great identification feature. Yellowlegs also have long necks and a white
rump (seen in flight or when stretching). They are lovely to
watch as they wade through puddles, ponds, sewage lagoons, and
mudflats looking for invertebrate prey. Both Lesser and Greater
Yellowlegs breed in Ontario's boreal forest and the Hudson Bay
Lowlands. Though they don't nest in trees as Solitary Sandpipers
do, Lesser Yellowlegs still perch in treetops, especially when they
are screaming at intruders to stay away from their hard-to-find
fledglings. Call is a one- or two-part *tew-tew*.

White below and mottled brown above,
with indistinct eye ring or "spectacles,"
longish straight beak, and longish finely
streaked neck. Legs long and yellow.

In flight or when stretching wing, note white rump and
finely barred tail. Same pattern on Greater Yellowlegs.

Greater Yellowlegs

Grand Chevalier

Tringa melanoleuca

L 29-33 CM (11-13 IN) | **WS** 59-61 CM (23-24 IN)

The Greater Yellowlegs is a bigger version of the Lesser Yellow-legs. If the two species stand close together, this can be easy enough to see, but if they are apart, you will need other clues. The best field mark is the beak. On the Greater, it is longer in proportion to its head size and usually slightly upturned. On the Lesser, it's usually straighter and shorter. Flight calls can also help. The Greater makes a loud three- or four-part *TEW TEW TEW!* The Lesser has a softer one- or two-part *tew-tew*.

White below and mottled brown above, with indistinct eye ring or "spectacles," long slightly upturned beak, long finely streaked neck, and long yellow legs. Breeding bird darker.

In flight, note large white rump and finely barred tail. Yellow feet project past tail.

Willet

Chevalier semipalmé

Tringa semipalmata

L 33–41 CM (13–16 IN) | **WS** 68–71 CM (27–28 IN)

These large sandpipers are rare visitors to Ontario but usually seen every year, and they are definitely worth looking for. They look a bit like an overgrown, dull, chunky yellowlegs until they spread their wings, revealing a startling black-and-white pattern. Reading an Ontario bird alert or using eBird will help you know when a Willet is in the province, but it is likely that most Ontarians will see more Willets on east coast beaches during a southern winter holiday. Call is a high-pitched, almost gull-like *kill-ya*.

Mottled brown and greyish above and whitish below, with brown barring, long neck, long strong beak, and pale "spectacles." Legs grey. Spread wings show bold black-and-white pattern.

Wilson's Phalarope

Phalarope de Wilson

Phalaropus tricolor

L 22-24 CM (9-10 IN) | **WS** 39-43 CM (15-17 IN)

Not only are phalaropes polyandrous—that is, the females have
more than one mate—but the females are also more brightly
coloured. They compete with other females for mates, and once
the eggs are laid, they leave in search of a new mate. The male
then does all of the incubation and raises the offspring on his
own. The Wilson's Phalarope is the only phalarope that breeds,
though sparsely, in southern Ontario. Its call is an un-sand-
piper-like nasal *wah* or grunting clucks.

Breeding female has grey cap and
long, very thin beak. Thick black eye
line blends into rich chestnut and
rufous neck. Back grey and chestnut,
underparts pale, legs black. In flight,
note all-white rump. (Breeding male
much less colourful.)

Juvenile has brown upperparts and
white or buffy underparts. Feathers on
upperparts have light edging. Pale
face with indistinct eye line. Legs
yellow. (Non-breeding adult similar,
but upperparts pale grey.)

Red-necked Phalarope

Phalarope à bec étroit

Phalaropus lobatus

L 16-20 CM (6-8 IN) | **WS** 32-34 CM (12-14 IN)

Phalaropes are the most aquatic shorebirds. They often swim like ducks while foraging (providing an excellent identification clue, as other shorebirds are less likely to do this), and they even have specially adapted lobed toes with webbing that help them paddle in open water. They are so well adapted to life on the water that most Red-necked and Red Phalaropes spend up to nine months a year at sea, returning to land only to nest in spring. Both species can sometimes be found in southern Ontario during migration, and Red-necked Phalaropes breed in the Hudson Bay Lowlands. Call is a series of harsh chattering notes.

Breeding female smudgy dark grey with white throat, reddish-chestnut neck, white crescent above eye, and very thin beak, as well as some light brown streaks on back. Legs dark. (Breeding male much paler.)

Non-breeding bird grey above and white below, with dark ear patch and very thin beak. (Juvenile similar, but brown replaces grey.)

Red Phalarope

Phalarope à bec large
Phalaropus fulicarius

L 19-21 cm (7-8 in) | **WS** 38-42 cm (15-17 in)

If you find a phalarope that is feeding, watch it carefully.
As it swims, it will turn in tight circles, creating a miniature upwelling that draws tiny invertebrates to the water's
surface, where the bird can grab them. Recent studies have
shown that phalaropes don't pick up individual invertebrates
and then throw them backwards into their mouth, as a heron
might. Instead, the shorebirds open their beak slightly, causing
food-carrying water droplets to travel up to their mouth via
surface tension. By doing this rapidly, they can eat many tiny
crustaceans fast and efficiently. The Red Phalarope's call is
high-pitched *peet*.

Breeding female has reddish-chestnut breast, brown body, black cap, and white cheek patch. Very rare in Ontario.

Non-breeding bird has grey upperparts, white underparts, and dark cheek patch. Beak thicker than Red-necked Phalarope.

Parasitic Jaeger

Labbe parasite

Stercorarius parasiticus

L 37–53 CM (14–21 IN) | **WS** 107–118 CM (42–47 IN)

This Arctic predator breeds in the Hudson Bay Lowlands, in the farthest reaches of Ontario. Its name reflects one of its hunting strategies: chasing down gulls or terns to steal the food they have caught. The jaeger shows a brazen personality when defending its nest as well and doesn't hesitate to dive-bomb humans who come too close. Parasitic Jaegers usually stick to the open ocean when they aren't nesting, but the Great Lakes attract a few in fall. The best places to find one are Kettle Point on Lake Huron, Point Edward in Sarnia, and Van Wagner's Beach in Hamilton. Go when there are strong onshore winds. The smaller Long-tailed Jaeger and larger Pomarine Jaeger are also possible.

In flight, note long, pointed, dark wings, pointed central tail feathers, and white in bases of primary feathers. Light-morph bird has dark upperparts and white underparts with dark collar. (Dark morph all dark, but primaries have white bases.) Immature jaeger usually brownish with dark barring and prominent white patches at base of primaries. Central tail feathers shorter than on adult.

Black-legged Kittiwake

Mouette tridactyle

Rissa tridactyla

L 38–41 CM (15–16 IN) | **WS** 94 CM (37 IN)

Gull enthusiasts may like to watch for rare gulls at dumps but are unlikely to spot a Black-legged Kittiwake there. A bird of the Arctic and salt water, it prefers sites with open water and usually shows up in Ontario only during fall migration. One of the most consistent places to find one is along the Niagara River, often at the bottom of Niagara Falls, in late fall. Sarnia and Hamilton are good places to look, too. Migrating kittiwakes in Ontario are usually immature birds, distinguished by the dark band on their nape.

In flight, watch for distinctive black patch on nape, dark M across upper wings, and dark band on tail. Beak and legs dark, with dark ear smudge.

In flight, non-breeding adult has grey upper wings and white under wings. Wings have black tips, as if dipped in ink. Beak yellow. Legs black, with dark ear smudge.

Ivory Gull

Mouette blanche

Pagophila eburnea

L 40–43 CM (16–17 IN) | **WS** 108–120 CM (42–47 IN)

The Canadian population of the Endangered Ivory Gull, an Arctic breeder, is currently only 30 percent of what it was in the 1980s. Climate change and toxins are likely major factors in the decline. Ivory Gulls are rare visitors to Ontario, and most sightings are of immature birds discovered in late fall and early winter. Unlike other rare gulls, which often occur in flocks of more common gull species, Ivory Gulls are usually found on their own. May give a high-pitched nasal whistle as well as tern-like calls.

Immature all white with dark spots and dark face. Legs short and black.

Adult all white. Beak greyish green with yellow tip. Legs black.

Sabine's Gull

Mouette de Sabine

Xema sabini

L 27-35 (10-14 IN) | **WS** 81-87 CM (32-35 IN)

Good news: A Sabine's Gull in breeding plumage is one of
the most beautiful gulls in the world. Bad news: Gulls in this
plumage are rarely seen in Ontario, but the juvenile birds that
do show up sport one of the most striking wing patterns in the
gull family, a combination of black, white, and brown triangles.
The gull breeds in the Arctic and spends its winters on the open
ocean but can be seen on the Great Lakes during migration,
mostly in fall. Watch for it with onshore winds in September
and October at Van Wagner's Beach in Hamilton or Point Pelee
National Park with southwest winds. Watch in October and
November along the Niagara River.

In flight, note juvenile's brown
cap and back and combination
of brown, white, and black
triangles on upper wing.
Slightly forked tail has black
tip.

Breeding adult has dark grey
hood with black ring at base,
dark beak with yellow tip, and
combination of grey, white, and
black triangles on upper wing.
Tail slightly forked.

Bonaparte's Gull

Mouette de Bonaparte

Chroicocephalus philadelphia

L 28-38 CM (11-15 IN) | **WS** 76-80 CM (30-32 IN)

The most common of our "hooded" gulls, the Bonaparte's often occurs in a flock of hundreds. Don't miss the opportunity to scan through a dense mass of whirling, diving birds as they forage, as doing so will improve your chances of finding a rare gull. The wing tips are the most important parts to study: Bonaparte's Gulls have a white wedge on the upper and lower part of their wings. This field mark is especially noticeable on adults. Call is raspy, like a combination of a tern and larger gull.

Small. Breeding gull has black hood, broken white eye ring, and dark beak as well as white triangle on wing tip and black tips on primaries. Legs reddish. (Non-breeding bird lacks hood, has dark smudge on ear.)

Immature gull has dark M on upper wings, dark trailing edge on wings, and white head with dark smudge on ear. Tail has black tip. Legs pale.

Black-headed Gull

Mouette rieuse

Chroicocephalus ridibundus

L 34–37 CM (13–15 IN) | **WS** 100–110 CM (39–43 IN)

Let's pretend that all Black-headed Gulls are named Waldo.
And where is he? Look in the flock of hundreds and hundreds of
Bonaparte's Gulls! On the Niagara River, this is a long-standing
tradition for many birders. Success depends all on the wings:
where the Bonaparte's is white under the primaries, the Black-
headed has a dark patch. Black-headed Gulls started breeding
in Newfoundland in 1977, and so far none have bred in Ontario.
Most of the world's population live in Europe and Asia; less
than one percent nests or overwinters in Canada.

Non-breeding gull has white head with dark
smudge on ear and red beak. Primary
feathers have black tips. White triangle on
wing tip, dark triangle on underpart of inner
primaries. Legs reddish. (Immature gull has
dark M on upper wings. Dark tip on tail.)

Breeding bird has darkish brown hood and
broken eye ring. Beak reddish.

Little Gull

Mouette pygmée

Hydrocoloeus minutus

L 28–30 CM (11–12 IN) | **WS** 61 CM (24 IN)

The compact Little Gull, a Eurasian species, has the distinction of being the smallest gull in the world. It is often spotted in flocks of Bonaparte's Gulls, where the adults' conspicuously dark under wings make them stand out. A nest found in 1962 at Oshawa's Second Marsh was the first place the gull bred in North America. Since then, only 32 additional nests have been discovered in the province. Watch for Little Gulls during migration along the shores of Lake Erie and Lake Ontario. The gull capital of the world, the Niagara River, is a great spot to find the bird in late autumn or early winter. Calls are higher pitched than those of a Bonaparte's Gull.

Adult winter has dark cap, dark smudge on ear, thin beak, and grey upperparts. White trailing edge runs from base of wings to round wing tips. Under wings dark. (Second-winter gull similar, but with lighter under wings and some black in primaries. Breeding adult has black head with no white near eye.) First-winter gull has dark cap, dark smudge on ear, dark M pattern on upper wings, and light under wings. Tail has black tip.

Ross's Gull

Mouette rosée

Rhodostethia rosea

L 28-31 CM (11-12 IN) | **WS** 90-100 CM (35-39 IN)

An endangered Arctic gull, the Ross's Gull sports a distinctive dark neck ring and a pinkish blush on the breast during the breeding season, and even when the bird is not in summer garb, its wedge-shaped tail is still noticeable in flight. The gull also has a very short beak, making it look rather dove-like. Ross's Gulls are quite rare in Ontario, but it is important to know what they look like, especially when searching for Little Gulls in a flock of Bonaparte's Gulls in November or December.

In flight, note grey under wings, not as dark as adult Little Gull. Wedge-shaped tail distinctive in all plumages.

Very small. Breeding adult has thin black neck ring, variable pinkish blush on breast, very short black beak, and red legs. (Non-breeding adult similar but lacks neck ring and has little, if any, blush. First-winter gull patterned like first-winter Little Gull but without cap.)

Laughing Gull

Mouette atricille

Leucophaeus atricilla

L 39–46 CM (15–18 IN) | **WS** 92–120 CM (36–47 IN)

To see a Laughing Gull in breeding plumage, Ontario birders usually have to head to the coast. The dark-hooded gull breeds along Atlantic shorelines from New Brunswick south to Florida, Mexico, and Central America as well as in the Caribbean, and it visits Ontario only rarely. Most sightings are at Lake Erie harbours, but it can also show up along Lake Ontario and Lake Huron shores, and even over inland rivers and lakes. This may occur outside of the breeding season when its characteristic hood is much reduced, just grey streaks on the back of its head.

Breeding bird has black hood, broken eye ring, and red beak. Upper wing dark grey with black, not white, wing tips.

First-winter gull has smudgy partial hood, dark beak, smudgy breast, and grey back. Wings brown wings with dark tips.

Franklin's Gull

Mouette de Franklin

Leucophaeus pipixcan

L 32-36 CM (12-14 IN) | **WS** 85-95 CM (33-37 IN)

The Franklin's Gull is a bird of the prairie region well known to forage on insects, mice, and other prey exposed by farm machinery in agricultural fields. It can be seen in the Rainy River/Lake of the Woods area, near the Minnesota border, in late summer and early fall, and it also shows up as a rarity in other parts of Ontario during migration. Watch for it in congregations of other gulls at hot spots such as the Niagara River and sewage lagoons.

Breeding adult has dark hood and thick, broken, white eye ring and may have pink blush on breast. White band separates dark wing tips from grey wings. Beak dark red.

First-summer (shown) and non-breeding gull have partial hood.

Ring-billed Gull

Goéland à bec cerclé

Larus delawarensis

L 43–54 CM (17–21 IN) | **WS** 105–117 CM (41–46 IN)

This and the Herring Gull are Ontario's most common gull species, and they present one of the biggest identification challenges. The adult Ring-billed Gull has a characteristic ring on its beak, but so, too, does the third-year Herring Gull. Fortunately, an adult Ring-billed has yellow legs, while the Herring has pink legs, and if the gulls appear together, you can see that the Ring-billed is much smaller than the Herring Gull.

Adult shows black wing tips with white windows.

Medium-sized gull. Breeding adult has
yellow beak with black ring, yellow eye, grey
mantle, black wing tips, and yellow legs.
(Non-breeding gull has streaking on nape.)

First-year gull has grey back, wings
with dark and light patches, pale
beak with dark tip, whitish rump,
dark tail tip, and pale pinkish legs.

Herring Gull

Goéland argenté

Larus argentatus

L 60–66 CM (24–26 IN) | **WS** 137–146 CM (54–58 IN)

The Herring Gull is a four-year gull. This means it takes four years for it to acquire adult plumage. (The Ring-billed Gull is a three-year gull.) Gulls can be tricky to identify because they wear many different plumages. Learning the field marks of the easier-to-identify adult gulls first will allow you to recognize important variations in size, beak shape, and flight style that are not dependent on age when you come across a flock that may have many species and many age groups in it.

Large. Breeding adult has yellow beak with red spot, yellow eye, grey mantle, black wing tips, and pink legs.

Adult in winter shows black wing tips with white windows and streaks on nape.

First-year gull has brown back and wings with dark and light patches. Beak all dark or pale with dark tip. Rump brown and mottled. Tail dark. Legs pale pinkish.

California Gull

Goéland de Californie

Larus californicus

L 47–54 CM (18–22 IN) | **WS** 130 CM (51 IN)

This gull normally breeds and spends the winters in the western half of North America, but it shows up in Ontario every year, often in flocks of Herring and Ring-billed Gulls. Gull aficionados scan through the birds comparing mantle colour: on the California Gull, it's a shade darker than the Herring and Ring-billed Gulls it may be sitting beside, making it stand out. In addition, its eyes are dark, while the eyes of Herring and Ring-billed Gulls are yellow.

Medium-sized gull. Adult in winter has yellow beak with red and black ring, dark eye, and dark smudgy streaks on head and nape. Mantle darkish grey, wing tips black, legs yellow. (Breeding bird has fully white head.)

Slaty-backed Gull

Goéland à manteau ardoisé

Larus schistisagus

L 55–69 CM (21–27 IN) | **WS** 132–160 CM (52–63 IN)

The Slaty-backed Gull is a large gull of the east coast of Asia that likes to wander. It was first found in Ontario in 1992 on the Niagara River, and its appearance in the province has recently become an annual affair, a reminder of the importance of scrutinizing every dark-mantled member of every flock. Features to watch for in winter are a smudgy eye patch and a distinctive row of white spots on the wing tips, known as the "string of pearls," visible when the gull is flying. Watch for it in large groups of fall and winter gulls, including those at landfills.

Large. Adult has yellow eye and yellow beak with red spot. Winter bird often has significant darkish streaks through eye and on nape (usually more than this individual). Mantle dark grey (not as dark as Great Black-backed). Legs pink. In flight, note "string of pearls" created by white spots between dark grey shafts and black tips of outer primary feathers. Dark flight feathers show through on under wing, similar to Lesser Black-backed and Great Black-backed Gulls.

Lesser Black-backed Gull

Goéland brun

Larus fuscus

L 51–64 CM (20–25 IN) | **WS** 124–150 CM (49–59 IN)

As numbers of the Lesser Black-backed Gull rise, it is being
seen in southern Ontario much more commonly. Look for a
gull that is slightly smaller than a Herring Gull and whose
mantle is almost as dark as that of a Great Black-backed. It
has yellow legs (the Great Black-backed has pink legs) and in
winter usually has quite a bit of streaking on its head and nape.
When a Lesser Black-backed and a Herring Gull stand together,
notice that the Lesser Black-backed is less chunky and shorter.
It has not been found nesting in Ontario yet.

Adult in summer has dark
grey mantle with black
wing tips.

Winter adult has dark
grey mantle with black
wing tips, yellow eye,
yellow beak with red spot,
yellow legs, and streaks
on head and nape (often
more than shown on this
individual).

Great Black-backed Gull

Goéland marin

Larus marinus

L 71–79 CM (28–31 IN) | **WS** 146–160 CM (57–63 IN)

The Great Black-backed Gull is the largest gull in the world and capable of swallowing big fish, ducklings, even young rabbits whole. Its bulky size and very dark mantle make it easy to pick out in a flock of gulls and distinguish it in any plumage from the Herring Gulls and Ring-billed Gulls with which it is often seen. A visit to a productive landfill or gull-covered shoreline will often reveal at least one of these magnificent birds.

In flight, note very dark grey mantle and black wing tips, and that white spot on outermost primary feather extends to tip (not seen on Lesser Black-backed Gull). Body very bulky.

Summer adult has very dark grey mantle, black wing tips, yellow eye, and yellow beak with red spot. Legs pink. Winter bird has only slight streaking on head and nape.

Iceland Gull

Goéland arctique

Larus glaucoides

L 50-60 CM (19-24 IN) | **WS** 115-137 CM (45-54 IN)

The smaller of our two "white-winged gulls," the Iceland Gull is a bit smaller than a Herring Gull. Its wing tips can be anywhere from dark grey to pure white, though most Icelands that show up in Ontario have some grey. A subspecies, the "Thayer's Gull," was once considered a separate species; it has black in its wing tips, though much less than a Herring Gull. Looking down at the Niagara River's Sir Adam Beck Generating Station into a swirling November flock of Herring Gulls and trying to pick out the Iceland Gulls is a rite of passage for any birder in Ontario.

Winter adult has pale grey mantle and usually some (variable) smudgy grey in wing tips. Beak yellow with red spot. Eyes usually yellowish (but could be dark). Legs pink.

Summer adult "Thayer's" subspecies has grey mantle. Wing tips have reduced black above (compared to Herring Gull) and grey below. Yellow beak with red spot. Usually dark eyes"

Glaucous Gull

Goéland bourgmestre

Larus hyperboreus

L 66-69 CM (26-27 IN) | **WS** 149-182 CM (59-72 IN)

The Glaucous Gull is the larger of our two "white-winged gulls";
the adult has pure white wing tips. It is much larger than a
Herring Gull and almost as large as a Great Black-backed Gull,
making it North America's second-biggest gull. The Glaucous
Gull is often found in congregations of other gulls in migration
and in winter. A dump is often a good place to look. It breeds
from Alaska to Labrador and may have bred once in Polar Bear
Provincial Park, along the Hudson Bay coast in Ontario.

Adult in summer has pale grey mantle
and fully white wing tips. Body large and
bulky. Eye yellow. Beak yellow with red
spot. Legs pink. Winter adult has streaks
on head and nape.

First-year gull all white with pale
brownish wash. Pink beak with dark tip.
(First-year Iceland Gull usually has
all-dark beak, but second-year gull can
have dark tip.) Legs pink.

Caspian Tern

Sterne caspienne

Hydroprogne caspia

L 47–54 CM (18–22 IN) | **WS** 120–135 CM (47–53 IN)

The largest tern in the world, the Caspian Tern is found everywhere but Antarctica. In Ontario, it usually breeds within colonies of Ring-billed Gulls, where it uses its large size to protect its young and eggs from untrustworthy neighbours. Most nesting sites in the province are along the Great Lakes. Seen at a distance, the tern is more often confused with a gull than another tern species—but look at that large orange beak! Makes a grating call that is lower pitched than that made by other terns.

Summer adult has grey upperparts, white underparts, large dark orange beak, and black cap. Winter adult has white flecking on forehead. Black legs.

Wing tips of adult in summer much darker underneath than above. Large orange beak visible at distance.

Black Tern

Guifette noire

Chlidonias niger

L 23-26 CM (9-10 IN) | **WS** 57-60 CM (22-24 IN)

The Black Tern is easy to identify because its black body and silvery wings are unlike our other mostly white terns. It breeds in southern Ontario and the Lake of the Woods area and is sometimes found in small colonies of fewer than 20 pairs. Preferring marshes, it builds its nest on floating material or muddy islands in open water. Makes high, harsh, whiny, one- or two-part barks.

Adult in summer has black body with white undertail coverts, grey wings and tail, and thin black beak.

Tern in winter has white underparts and white head with dark hindcrown and ear patch.

Common Tern

Sterne pierregarin

Sterna hirundo

L 31-38 CM (12-15 IN) | **WS** 75-80 CM (29-32 IN)

The Common Tern, Forster's Tern, and Arctic Tern pose identification challenges in Ontario. The Arctic Tern breeds along the Hudson Bay coastline, so most birders rarely see it, yet it can sometimes be found along the Ottawa River in late May and early June. The Common Tern breeds in colonies along many Great Lakes shorelines, as well as along the Saint Lawrence River and some inland waterways. Makes a harsh, throaty, two-part call.

Summer adult has black cap and red beak with dark tip. (Arctic Tern has shorter beak without dark tip.) Wings grey above and whiter underneath with dark trailing edge on primary tips. Thin black outer tail feathers can be hard to see.

Winter adult has more dark grey on trailing edge of upper primaries. Forehead white. Beak dark.

Forster's Tern

Sterne de Forster

Sterna forsteri

L 33-36 cm (13-14 in) │ **WS** 79 cm (31 in)

The Forster's Tern prefers to nest in marshy habitats more than the Common Tern and is mostly restricted to a few nesting sites along the shores of Lake Erie and Lake Saint Clair. A heavier orange beak with a black tip, whiter primaries, and a longer tail distinguish the Forster's Tern. In addition, its outer tail feathers are white, while they are black on the Common Tern. Winter adult Forster's Terns also have a distinctive black ear patch. Call is similar to Common Tern but shorter, lower, and not as harsh.

Summer adult has black cap. Beak orange with black tip. Wings light grey above with whitish primaries and dark trailing edge on undersides of primaries. Long forked tail has white outer edges and dark inner edges.

First-year tern (shown here) and adult in winter have duskier upper primaries (especially first-year). Dark ear patch. Dark beak.

Red-throated Loon

Plongeon catmarin

Gavia stellata

L 53–69 cm (21–27 in) | **WS** 100–120 cm (39–47 in)

To see a beautiful Red-throated Loon sitting on a waterside nest in Ontario, you will likely have to travel a long way: the loon nests only in the Hudson Bay Lowlands. But during migration and in winter, you can find it in southern Ontario on the Great Lakes and sometimes smaller bodies of water. In winter, it can be difficult to distinguish from other loons, but beak shape can be revealing. Red-throated Loons have a thin upward-pointing beak that differs from those of other loon species.

Winter adult has white head and neck with dark cap and nape. Fairly thin beak appears to turn slightly upwards. Back dark with white spots (often not easy to see). Flanks whitish.

Summer adult has grey head and striped nape, red throat, and white breast with stripes on sides. Back dark brownish grey.

Common Loon

Plongeon huard

Gavia immer

L 66-91 CM (26-36 IN) | **WS** 104-131 CM (41-52 IN)

The Common Loon is Ontario's provincial bird for many
reasons. One: It loves lakes. And since Ontario has its fair share
of wetlands, it's a perfect fit. Two: Its calls. It makes many
different haunting calls, including the wavering and fluid
tremolo, the mournful wail, and a high-pitched yodel. All are
definite wilderness sounds. Three: Well, look at it! Its black
breeding plumage is covered in intricate spots, stripes, and
squares of white. And while it may seem monochromatic, in
the right light the head glints with shiny greens and purples.
Everyone needs to spend some time with a Common Loon, pref-
erably while paddling a canoe or kayak on a northern lake.

Summer adult has black head and neck,
long, pointed, black beak, red eye, and
white necklace. Breast white with thin
black stripes on sides. Flanks and tail black
with small white dots. Back black with large
white squares.

Winter adult has brown head and neck,
white chin and throat blending with brown
of neck, suggestion of white necklace,
broken white eye ring, grey beak, and
white breast. Body and tail brown.

Double-crested Cormorant

Cormoran à aigrettes

Nannopterum auritum

L 70-90 CM (27-36 IN) | **WS** 114-123 CM (45-49 IN)

The Double-crested Cormorant probably has the coolest eyes of any Ontario bird. Set off against orange skin on the face and chin, and surrounded by an intricately patterned eye ring, the sea-green iris is truly a work of art. Top that off with a funky pig-tail hairdo and shining black plumage, and you have a winner of a bird. Double-crested Cormorants are common across southern Ontario and especially the Great Lakes, where they eat primarily invasive alewife and rainbow smelt. In colonies, they make a series of hollow, knocking croaks.

Summer adult black with black (or white) "horns" when breeding. Beak long and hooked, with bright orange skin at base. Eyes turquoise, with long neck and dark feet. First-year cormorant (inset) brown with pale throat and breast, long neck, and long, hooked, yellow-orange beak.

American White Pelican

Pélican d'Amérique

Pelecanus erythrorhynchos

L 127–165 CM (50–65 IN) | **WS** 244–290 CM (96–114 IN)

The Bald Eagle, Great Blue Heron, Trumpeter Swan, and
Sandhill Crane might vie for Ontario's widest wingspan, but
the American White Pelican is the clear winner. Its wingspan is
274 cm (9 ft). That's over two feet wider than the wings of any of
the four other species. The pelican uses its big wings to soar on
rising warm air currents while migrating to and from nesting
sites in central North America (including northwestern Ontario)
and overwintering sites in the southern states. Makes grunting
sounds at colonies.

Very large. Summer adult white with long
neck and extremely large orange beak,
which may have hornlike projection on top.
Legs and feet orange. In flight, note very
wide wingspan. White with black primaries
and outer secondaries and extremely large
orange beak. Tucks in neck.

American Bittern

Butor d'Amérique

Botaurus lentiginosus

L 60–68 CM (23–34 IN) | **WS** 92 CM (39 IN)

A master of camouflage, the American Bittern is coloured
perfectly to blend into a cattail marsh. It enhances its costume
by pointing its beak upwards and either staying perfectly still
or swaying slightly to mimic wind-blown cattails. Sometimes
the best way to detect it is to listen for its distinctive yet strange
call, which sounds like a stump being pounded into wet earth.
The vocalization has earned the bird fun names, such as "thunder
pumper," "stake driver," and "water belcher." American Bitterns
breed across all of Ontario where suitable wetlands occur.

Finely marked brown upperparts
and light-coloured but streaked
underparts. Thick black streak
on side of neck. Often holds
long pointed beak upright.

Least Bittern

Petit Blongios

Ixobrychus exilis

L 28-36 CM (11-14 IN) | **WS** 41-46 CM (16-18 IN)

When birders first see a Least Bittern, many think they have found a baby American Bittern. The Least is the world's smallest heron, and so light it can walk through cattails by holding onto their leaves. If disturbed, it will behave like any bittern, pointing its beak to the sky in an attempt to blend in. Least Bitterns are found in southern Ontario marshlands, but a few may be found in northwestern Ontario as well. The extensive marshes in southwestern Ontario present the best chances for sightings: Point Pelee, Long Point, Rondeau, Hillman Marsh, and Lake Saint Clair. The song of a Least Bittern is a series of *cu-cu-cu-cu* notes that are very cuckoo-like.

Very small, with dark cap and back (male shown, lighter on female) and orangey-buff face, neck, and wings. Underparts white with streaks.

Great Blue Heron

Grand Héron

Ardea herodias

L 97–137 cm (38–54 in) | **WS** 167–201 cm (66–79 in)

The Great Blue Heron's size allows it to hunt a wide variety
of animals. It has been known to catch and swallow whole not
only frogs and fish but also very large prey, including an adult
Least Bittern and a fully grown grey squirrel. The heron can be
found from Ontario's southern tip north to James Bay. In spring,
watch for multiple large stick nests in close proximity in failing
or dead trees. Colonies can have as many as 150 nests, though
the average is closer to 35. Take care not to disturb a colony, as
frightened chicks may fall out of nests or leave prematurely.
Gives a harsh, bark-like croak in flight.

Our largest heron. Adult steel
grey with white head, orange
beak, and black head stripe
and head plumes. Throat
whitish with dark streaks.
Shoulder black. In flight, tucks
in head, and legs trail behind.
Slow, heavy wingbeats. Large
wings often bowed.

Great Egret

Grande Aigrette
Ardea alba

L 94–104 CM (37–41 IN) | **WS** 131–145 CM (51–57 IN)

Numbers of this southern heron are increasing in Ontario, much to the delight of birders. Expansion into southern Canada is a great sign that the species continues to rebound from exploitation in the late 1800s and early 1900s, when hunting for the fashion industry caused the North American population to decrease more than 95 percent. Efforts to spare this and other birds from hunting pressure continue to this day, and the Great Egret is proudly displayed on the logo of the National Audubon Society. Call is a low, rough croak.

Large. Breeding adult all white with yellow beak, green face, and long plumes over tail. Legs and feet black. In flight, tucks in head, and long legs trail behind. In breeding season, plumes extend past tail.

Green Heron

Héron vert

Butorides virescens

L 41-46 CM (16-18 IN) | **WS** 64-68 CM (25-27 IN)

Chow! If you hear that sound, look up! You may glimpse a Green Heron flying from one hiding spot to another. When foraging, it is often found along the scrubby edges of ponds and ditches. Watch it carefully, as it may use a piece of bait to attract a fish close enough to catch. The behaviour is considered an example of true tool use, something that once defined what it is to be human. Green Herons breed across southern Ontario, building nests out of sticks or aquatic vegetation in a wide variety of situations: deciduous trees or shrubs, coniferous trees (including those in plantations), or in marshes.

Small, with dark cap, chestnut neck, white throat, and greenish-grey body. Short orangish legs. In flight, looks stubby for a heron. Makes deep wingbeats with short wings, and short legs trail behind.

Black-crowned Night-Heron

Bihoreau gris

Nycticorax nycticorax

L 58-66 CM (23-26 IN) | **WS** 115-118 CM (45-47 IN)

The Black-crowned Night-Heron will forage during the day, but most hunting happens at night. Its genus, *Nycticorax*, means "night-crow," reflecting both its nocturnal habits and its flight call, which sounds crow-like. In Ontario, we also sometimes see North America's rarer night-heron, the Yellow-crowned Night-Heron, which is greyer and has a boldly striped head. (Immatures of the two species can be much trickier to tell apart.) During breeding season, Black-crowned Night-Herons occur mostly along the shores of Lake Ontario, Lake Erie, Lake Huron/Georgian Bay, and the Saint Lawrence River, though a few nest inland.

Short and stocky. Adult has black cap, dark beak, red eye, and white face, throat, and underparts. Back black. Wings and tail grey. Legs yellow. Immature (below) streaky brown. Eye yellow to orange. White streaks on back, white spots on wings.

Black Vulture

Urubu noir

Coragyps atratus

L 60–68 CM (23–27 IN) | **WS** 137–150 CM (54–59 IN)

Scan all flocks of Turkey Vultures you see along the Niagara River for Black Vultures, which have become regular inhabitants of the area recently. Unlike the Turkey Vulture, the Black Vulture does not hunt by smell; it relies on vision both to find carrion to eat and to watch for Turkey Vultures that might be descending to a meal. Once on the ground, it can bully its cousin off a carcass, even though it is smaller. Ontario's first Black Vulture nest has not been recorded yet.

Adult holds wide wings in slight dihedral or V when soaring, flaps fast and shallow, and has short triangular tail and small, naked, grey head. Light grey primary feathers contrast with black wings and body. Long beak with light tip. Grey legs.

Turkey Vulture

Urubu à tête rouge

Cathartes aura

L 64-81 CM (25-32 IN) | **WS** 170-178 CM (67-70 IN)

The Turkey Vulture could be called gross. It eats mostly dead animals that it finds by smell and, even in flight, can detect carrion hidden beneath the forest canopy. Its head is bald, so no feathers get gummed up when it reaches inside a carcass. It defends itself at the nest by vomiting at the intruder. And it cools off by pooping on its own legs. But such attributes are easily forgotten when one takes to the air, circling gracefully upwards with barely a flap. Makes a hissing sound at the nest.

Adult has long tail and small, naked, red head. (Young bird has grey head.) Holds wings in strong dihedral or V when soaring and rocks or teeters in flight. Wingbeats deep and heavy. Grey flight feathers contrast with black wing linings and body. Body blackish with some brown wash or edging on back and wings. Long tail and pale pinkish legs.

Golden Eagle

Aigle royal

Aquila chrysaetos

L 70–84 CM (27–33 IN) | **WS** 185–220 CM (73–87 IN)

This is one of our most misidentified raptors. Many birders
think a big brown eagle without a white head and tail must
be a Golden Eagle, yet most of these sightings are immature
Bald Eagles. There's an easy way to tell flying birds apart,
though: look at the wing linings. Golden Eagles have all-dark
wing linings, while immature Bald Eagles usually have at least
some white mottling. In southern Ontario, Golden Eagles are
most likely to be seen from late October to early November
from hawk migration sites on the north shore of Lake Erie.
The eagles build cliffside nests in the Hudson Bay Lowlands, in
northern Ontario. May give a repeated high-pitched *kee-up* call.

Large. Adult has dark brown body, all-dark wing
linings, and lightly barred wing and tail flight
feathers. Golden nape hard to see in flight.
Immature (shown) similar but has variable amounts
of white at base of flight feathers on wings and tail.

Bald Eagle

Pygargue à tête blanche

Haliaeetus leucocephalus

L 71–96 CM (28–38 IN) | **WS** 204 CM (80 IN)

Nothing compares to the thrill of watching an adult Bald Eagle glide overhead on a crisp January day. Populations once crashed due to chemical contaminants such as DDT but have been recovering for decades. Now the majestic bird breeds throughout the province, and many eagles overwinter along open rivers throughout southern Ontario, to the delight of birders and non-birders alike. While TV commercials often pair the Red-tailed Hawk's rough descending scream with the image of a soaring Bald Eagle, the eagle's call is a jumble of whiny whistles.

Adult has very long wide wings and holds them flat or in slight dihedral or V. Makes fairly stiff, slow wingbeats. Head large and white, with very heavy yellow beak. Body and wings brown. Tail and undertail coverts white. Immature (right) dark brown with variable white mottling.

Northern Harrier

Busard des marais

Circus hudsonius

L 46-50 cm (18-20 in) | **WS** 102-118 cm (40-47 in)

Our most graceful raptor, the Northern Harrier is a master of looking for prey while flying just above the ground. Like the Turkey Vulture, it hold its wings in a stiff V in flight, and it has a wonderful field mark that can be seen at a distance: a bright white rump patch. Preferring open areas such as wet meadows, agricultural fields, and marshes, it nests on the ground in dense cover. Its breeding range covers all of Ontario. May give a high-pitched *kek-kek-kek-kek-kek*.

In flight, usually holds wings in strong dihedral or V and teeters. Wings and tail long. Male has smoky grey head and upper breast, white belly, undertail coverts, and under wings, and black wing tips. Tail grey with thick dark band near tip. Rump white.

Adult female has brown head and body with buffy underparts and wing linings with dark streaks. Primaries, secondaries, and tail feathers banded. Rump white. (First-year bird has orangish wash on breast and wing linings.)

Northern Goshawk

Autour des palombes

Accipiter gentilis

L 53–64 CM (20–26 IN) | **WS** 103–117 CM (40–47 IN)

Because the mighty Northern Goshawk is so impressive looking, everyone should see at least one, but only from a distance. As any experienced ornithologist or naturalist will tell you, failing to heed the hawk's repeated screamed warnings that you are too close to a nest may get you chased and possibly struck. Northern Goshawks have started nesting in agreement forests and other conifer plantations in various places in southern Ontario, so you may not have to go too far to find one. Alarm call is a loud *kak-kak-kak-kak-kak-kak!*

Adult has dark crown, thick eye line, thick white eyebrow, and red eyes. Back, wings, and tail slate grey. Very thin grey barring on white breast and belly. Undertail coverts white. First-year goshawk has thin eyebrow, yellow eyes, and brown back and wings, possibly with some whitish patches. Long tail with thick dark jagged bars. Thick brown streaks on buffy or whitish breast, belly, and undertail coverts.

Sharp-shinned Hawk

Épervier brun

Accipiter striatus

L 24-34 CM (9-13 IN) | **WS** 43-57 CM (17-24 IN)

Nothing causes birds to explode from a backyard feeder like the sudden appearance of a Sharp-shinned or Cooper's Hawk. Telling the adults of the two species apart is often a challenge. A male Sharp-shinned is jay sized, while a female Cooper's is crow sized, but the size of a female Sharp-shinned and a male Cooper's can be similar. If you can make neither heads nor tails of a perched adult hawk, look at the head and tail. On a Sharp-shinned, the tail feathers are all the same length, while on a Cooper's, the outer feathers are shorter than the central feathers. Also, the Sharp-shinned's head is small, rounded, and more dove-like, while the head of a Cooper's is large and slightly crested or squarish, with a fierce expression. The Sharp-shinned's call is a high-pitched *kek-kek-kek-kek-kek*.

Adult has bluish-grey back, wings, and tail, thick rusty-orange barring on white breast, belly, and wing linings, white undertail coverts, and dark bands on primaries, secondaries, and tail feathers. Tail tipped with thin white band. Eyes red. Holds rounded wings flat when soaring and pushes leading edge forward, causing small head to look tucked in. Wingbeats floppy. Tail long with squarish tip and thick dark bands. First-year hawk has thick brown streaks on white breast and belly. Bands on wings and tail.

Cooper's Hawk

Épervier de Cooper

Accipiter cooperii

L 37–45 CM (14–18 IN) | **WS** 62–90 CM (24–36 IN)

In southern Ontario, this is the accipiter that is most likely to zoom into your backyard and try to grab one of the birds fleeing in every direction. While it might be disturbing to see a Cooper's Hawk take a sparrow, dove, or other songbird, remember that predation is an important part of any ecological system. Planting conifers or dense shrubs nearby will give your feeder birds a place to escape and hide. The alarm call of the Cooper's is a loud *kak-kak-kak-kak-kak-kak!*

Adult has bluish-grey back, wings, and tail, thick rusty orange barring on white breast, belly, and wing linings, white undertail coverts, and dark bands on primaries, secondaries, and tail feathers. Eyes red.

First-year hawk has narrow brown streaks on white breast and belly. Bands on primaries and secondaries. Holds rounded wings flat when soaring. Long rounded tail with dark bars.

Red-shouldered Hawk

Buse à épaulettes

Buteo lineatus

L 43–61 CM (17–24 IN) | **WS** 94–111 CM (37–44 IN)

In many bird groups, particular parts of the body hold important clues to identification. For hawks in the genus *Buteo*, study the tail. Bands on the tail of the Red-shouldered Hawk appear in a thick-thin pattern — thick dark bands are separated by thin white bands. In contrast, bands on the Broad-winged Hawk's tail appear in a thick-thick pattern; the thick dark bands are separated by a thick white band. The Red-shouldered repeats a loud, screamed *keeyaah!*, sounding somewhat gull-like.

Rusty orange barring on white breast, belly, and wing linings, thin black bands on primaries and secondaries, and rufous patch on shoulder. Tail has thick dark and thin white bands and thin white band at tip.

First-year hawk has thick dark streaks on white breast and belly. Holds wide round-tipped wings flat or slightly drooped when soaring. Less distinct bands on primaries and secondaries. Dark tips on primaries. Translucent "windows" near tips of primaries. Broad tail has many thin dark bands.

Broad-winged Hawk

Petite Buse

Buteo platypterus

L 34-44 CM (13-17 IN) | **WS** 81-100 CM (32-40 IN)

The migration of our smallest buteo is one of the greatest spectacles in the natural world, and Ontario is a perfect place to witness it. In fall, the Great Lakes act like a giant funnel, causing Broad-winged Hawks retreating from the boreal forest to gather along the north shore of Lake Erie, where they circle together on rising currents of warm air, often in huge numbers, before gliding onward. On a September day in 1999, no fewer than 555,371 Broad-wingeds were counted as they moved from Ontario past Lake Erie Metro Park, just south of Detroit, Michigan. Nearby Holiday Beach and Hawk Cliff, near Port Stanley, are super places to watch. Call is a clear, very high-pitched, two-note whistle.

Adult has slightly pointed, wide wings, fairly short tail, rusty barring on white breast and belly, and white wing linings with a few rusty bars. Tips of primaries black. Wings have thick black trailing edge. (First year hawk has streaked breast and tail with many thin dark bars). Tail has two thick black bands separated by one thick white band, with thin white band at tip. Holds wings flat when soaring.

Rough-legged Hawk

Buse pattue

Buteo lagopus

L 47–52 CM (18–21 IN) | **WS** 132–138 CM (52–54 IN)

Rough-legged Hawks nest on the Arctic tundra and visit
Ontario in winter only. Striking plumage variation makes each
individual a little bit different. In flight, watch for Osprey-like
"wrist" patches that stand out on all but the dark-morph birds,
which are less common in the province than the light morphs.
Blackish-brown wing linings on dark birds contrast with
silvery-white flight feathers—certainly a memorable combination when seen on a flying bird lit up with sunlight reflecting
off snow. Call is a clear *keeeeyer*.

Pale-morph adult has pale
head and mottled upper breast.
Lower breast and belly has dark
mottling (usually male) or are
solid dark (usually female).
Undertail coverts white. Back
dark with white mottling. Tail
white with one or two narrow
dark bands and one thick dark
band near white tip. Great
variation in both sexes.

Wings long, wide, and rounded. Tail relatively long and broad. Wing linings light with dark mottling, dark "wrist" patches, and dark tips to primaries and secondaries. Mottled (or solid) dark belly band. Holds wings in dihedral or V.

Dark-morph hawk has very dark brown head, wing linings, and body, white primaries and secondaries, and dark tips on primaries and end of tail.

Red-tailed Hawk

Buse à queue rousse

Buteo jamaicensis

L 45–65 CM (18–26 IN) | **WS** 114–133 CM (45–53 IN)

Likely the most commonly seen raptor, the Red-tailed Hawk is prominent in winter along highways in any agricultural area, and it has also become regular in cities, hunting for squirrels and cottontails in neighbourhood parks. Immature hawks lack the characteristic red tail but are still fairly easy to identify, since bands on their tail appear in a thin pattern of very thin dark and thin light bands. It appears on no other buteo. The young birds also sport lovely dark marks on the leading edge of their wings, just like the adults; the Red-tailed is the only North American hawk to have them. Call is a well-known, rough, descending scream: *keee-aaaarrrrr!*

Adult has wide, long, rounded wings, short, broad, red tail, and whitish or buffy underparts with variable amounts of dark streaks on belly (often forming band). Holds wings in very shallow dihedral or V when soaring. First-year hawk similar but has yellow eyes and a thinly barred tail.

Osprey

Balbuzard pêcheur

Pandion haliaetus

L 54-58 CM (21-23 IN) | **WS** 105-180 CM (59-71 IN)

After a huge decline due to organochlorine pesticide use, the Osprey is back. And it is becoming common in many areas across the province, including city edges. Nesting on power poles, sport field lights, and cell towers, the Osprey can now be found in many places that have a lake or river as part of the landscape. Nothing is more humbling than spending a few hours in a boat or on a riverbank, unsuccessfully trying to catch a fish, and then seeing an Osprey dive and catch one right in front of you. Call is a repeated, high-pitched, clear whistle.

Adult holds long wings in downward curve, producing shallow M. Wings may bend at "wrist." Can look surprisingly gull-like at distance. May hover while hunting. Underparts white with possible streaked necklace. Flight feathers heavily barred, especially on secondaries. Dark "wrist" patches and finely barred tail. White head, thick dark brown eye line, and dark beak.

Barn Owl

Effraie des clochers

Tyto alba

L 32–40 CM (12–16 IN) | **WS** 100–125 CM (39–49 IN)

This owl belongs to a different family (Tytonidae) than our other owls, the so-called typical owls, and has a distinctive heart-shaped face. Very widespread, it is found on every continent except Antarctica. As its name suggests, it often uses human structures, such as barns, attics, and silos, for nesting sites. In fact, the loss of old barns might be a reason the species has become Endangered in Ontario. In 2007, it was estimated that only 5–10 pairs remained in the whole province. Gives a blood-curdling scream.

White heart-shaped face has dark eyes. Back buffy gold with grey mottling and small white and black spots. White underparts variably washed with buffy gold and small black spots. (Female usually darker.) Tail short, legs long.

Snowy Owl

Harfang des neiges

Bubo scandiacus

L 52-71 CM (22-28 IN) | **WS** 126-145 CM (49-57 IN)

Southern Ontario hosts Snowy Owls every winter, but some years, when the birds irrupt, or move south unpredictably, are better than others. An irruption seems to occur after a breeding season when prey such as lemmings are particularly common, allowing the owls to raise more young. In winter, there ends up being not enough food to go around, so more owls than normal come south, much to the delight of human observers. May make infrequent grunts or whistles on their wintering grounds.

All white. Adult male may have some dark or dusky spots.

Female and first-year male have variable black barring on crown, back, wings, breast, belly, and tail. Eyes yellow, tail short.

Great Horned Owl

Grand-duc d'Amérique

Bubo virginianus

L 46–63 CM (18–25 IN) | **WS** 101–145 CM (40–57 IN)

This tiger with wings is an apex predator that tends to focus on the most common medium-sized prey in its range, mostly mice, voles, and cottontail rabbits. But it is known to take much larger prey as well, including Great Blue Herons, Osprey, geese, skunks, and house cats (a good reason to keep your cat indoors). Great Horned Owls live across the entire province but are less common in the north than in the south, where it is our most common large owl (though it can still be surprisingly difficult to see). Call is a familiar, low *hoo hoo-hoo... hoooooooo hoooooooo.*

Has ear tufts (but can be flattened), orangey-brown facial disks with dark borders, and yellow eyes. Eyebrows, moustache, and throat patch whitish (can be concealed). Back mottled brownish grey, underparts buffy with thin dark barring. Tail short. (Northern birds can be significantly paler and greyer.) In flight, note very wide wings. Under wings buffy with dark comma on "wrist."

Long-eared Owl

Hibou moyen-duc

Asio otus

L 35–40 cm (14–16 in) | **WS** 90–110 cm (35–40 in)

The Long-eared Owl is much smaller than the Great Horned Owl but is so similar in markings that it may have evolved to mimic the larger, fiercer owl for protection. (Long-eared Owls in Europe and Asia, where Great Horneds don't occur, have orange eyes and tawnier plumages, features that are similar to those of the large Eurasian Eagle Owls that share their range.) The Long-eared Owl is nocturnal and so is most likely to be seen when a flock of noisy Black-capped Chickadees or Blue Jays betray its roosting spot in nearby conifers. Makes many different sounds, including squeals, hisses, and barks. Male's breeding call is a series of deep, evenly spaced hoots.

Has long ear tufts, yellow eyes, light eyebrows, orangey-brown facial disks with dark borders, and black vertical lines through eyes. Back mottled brownish grey. Underparts buffy with dark barring and streaking with some white mottling. Tail short.

Short-eared Owl
Hibou des marais
Asio flammeus

L 34–42 CM (13–17 IN) | **WS** 85–103 CM (33–41 IN)

The Short-eared Owl is possibly the most entertaining owl to watch because it hunts mostly at dusk and dawn and it prefers open fields and marshes, affording birders a ringside seat. The owl hunts on the wing, turning and diving quickly into the weeds when it finds a meadow vole or other prey. In areas with a high vole population, up to 30 or 40 Short-eareds can be seen hunting a once. Gives a series of deep hoots. Also does high-pitched barking notes and a raspy *kee-yaaaah*.

Slender owl with whitish or buffy facial disks, yellow eyes surrounded by black patch, and very short, centrally placed ear tufts (often hard to see). Back and wings brown with buffy or whitish mottling. Underparts whitish or buffy with brown streaks. Tail short.

Northern Hawk Owl

Chouette épervière

Surnia ulula

L 36–45 CM (14—18 IN) | **WS** 71 CM (28 IN)

The Northern Hawk Owl is well named. Its body is shaped like a hawk's; it has pointier wings, a longer tail, and a smaller head than most other owls. Even the rusty barring on its breast and belly is reminiscent of the colouration of a Cooper's or Sharp-shinned Hawk. And it is speedier than other owls as well. A boreal species, it sometimes comes to southern Ontario in the winter, where it becomes a favourite with birders. It makes a whistled trill similar to a Wilson's Snipe's winnowing.

Smallish head (for an owl) with light grey or white facial disks with thick black borders that extend to yellow eyes. Crown brownish grey with small white spots. White and black lines on sides of head. Back brownish with white mottling. Underparts white with rufous or brown barring. Tail long.

Barred Owl

Chouette rayée

Strix varia

L 43–50 CM (17–20 IN) | **WS** 99–110 CM (39–43 IN)

While the Barred Owl is beautiful, it is its distinctive call—sounding like *"Who cooks for you? Who cooks for you all?"*—that thrills lovers of dense woods and wild places. Campers listen for it in the middle of the night. And, if you are lucky, the owl might add excited cackles and laughs to the repertoire. The vocalizations have earned the bird the nicknames "laughing owl" and "crazy owl." The Barred Owl mostly nests across the central parts of Ontario, where it prefers continuous mixed deciduous and coniferous forests.

Facial disks have brown borders. Eyes dark. Upperparts brown with white mottling. Underparts white or buffy, breast barred. Thick dark streaks on belly. Tail short. Under wings buffy with dark comma on "wrist."

Great Gray Owl

Chouette lapone
Strix nebulosa

L 61–84 CM (24–33 IN) | **WS** 137–153 CM (54–60 IN)

While both the Great Horned Owl and the Snowy Owl weigh
more, the Great Gray Owl is our largest-looking owl. It is 26
inches long, and its huge facial disks make its stare something
to behold. Despite its hulking dimensions, it has small feet for
its size and usually eats only small mammals, such as voles. In
years when Great Gray Owls irrupt, or suddenly move south,
they often prove too popular. Hordes of people gather to see
them, putting the owls at risk. To protect them from disturbance, birders are encouraged not to report sightings on social
media and other public platforms. The Great Gray Owl gives a
series of very deep, booming hoots.

Large owl with yellow eyes
ringed by thin, dark,
concentric circles and large
facial disks with dark
borders. Eyebrows and
moustache light grey. Broken
white line across throat (can
be hard to see). Body grey
with dusky mottling.

Boreal Owl

Nyctale de Tengmalm

Aegolius funereus

L 21–25 CM (8–11 IN) | **WS** 55–58 CM (21–24 IN)

Most hawks and owls are sexually dimorphic: the females are larger than the males. In the Boreal Owl, this can be extreme: the heaviest female can weigh 215 g (7.6 oz), while the smallest male weighs only 93 g (3.3 oz). Since she spends more time at the nest while the male brings much of the food for the family, it's thought that her greater mass might help her defend her eggs and young against predators. The abundance of the owl is likely linked to the abundance of its favourite prey, the red-backed vole, whose population swells and falls on a four-year cycle. Boreal Owls tend to move south during winter about every four years, when vole populations are low. Makes a rapid series of short hollow whistles.

Adult has white or greyish facial disks with thick broken borders that extend to eyes on top and bottom. Eyes yellow. Forehead dark with white spots. Back brown with white spots. Underparts white with thick mottled streaks. Tail short.

Northern Saw-whet Owl

Petite Nyctale

Aegolius acadicus

L 18–21 cm (7–8 in) | **WS** 42–48 cm (16–19 in)

This is our smallest and, arguably, cutest owl; everyone remembers the first time they saw one. Birders usually learn of a Northern Saw-whet Owl's presence when chickadees, jays, or nuthatches find one roosting in a dense conifer. If you hear small birds making a ruckus together, it's always worth taking a peek. Hearing the owl's monotonous nighttime toot, toot, toot, toot, toot, toot is another way of knowing if one is around. On the breeding grounds, the Northern Saw-whet Owl often nests in old Pileated Woodpecker holes.

Tiny with brownish-streaked facial disks, yellow eyes, and brown forehead with short, thin, white streaks. Back and wings brown with white spots. Underparts white with thick rufous-brown streaks. Tail short.

Eastern Screech-Owl

Petit-duc maculé

Megascops asio

L 16–25 CM (6–10 IN) | **WS** 48–61 CM (19–24 IN)

Like a tiny Great Horned Owl, the Eastern Screech-Owl is a
generalist and will eat almost anything it can sink its talons
into. Pigeons, crayfish, earthworms, leeches, fish, grasshoppers,
and salamanders could all be added to its regular diet of small
rodents and songbirds. In Ontario, screech-owls occur in three
colours, or morphs: grey, rufous, or brown. On cold days and
especially in winter, watch for one sunning itself at the opening
of a natural tree cavity, an old woodpecker hole, or a Wood
Duck box. Makes two main calls: a modulating, mellow whistle,
and a shrill falling whinny.

Grey-morph owl has ear
tufts (can be flattened),
yellow eyes, and thin
black border to facial
disks. Eyebrows and
moustache white. Beak
pale yellowish green.
Upperparts grey with
dark mottling and white
spots, underparts white
with thin dark barring
and streaking. Tail short.

Belted Kingfisher

Martin-pêcheur d'Amérique

Megaceryle alcyon

L 28-35 cm (11-14 in) | **WS** 48-58 cm (19-23 in)

Noisy Belted Kingfishers let you know they're around with a loud rattle call. They can be found along the edge of any open water, and some even stick around in winter after most individuals have migrated south. In spring, they nest in burrows that they dig in the banks of rivers and lakes. Watch the next kingfisher you see hunting: Its beak-first dives into the water are spectacular, and the way it kills the fish it catches — by bashing them against its perch — shows that this is a mighty, though diminutive, predator. Belted Kingfishers are found throughout the province.

Steely blue above and white below with large double crest, long strong beak, and thick white neck ring. Blue breast band and rusty belt on female. Tail barred. Male lacks rusty belt.

Red-headed Woodpecker
Pic à tête rouge
Melanerpes erythrocephalus

L 19-23 CM (7-9 IN) | **WS** 42 CM (16-17 IN)

The Red-headed Woodpecker is a beautifully patterned bird and a favourite of all who see it. Unfortunately, between the 1980s and early 2000s, the Ontario population dropped by 64 percent, and the downward trend has continued. The woodpecker is now considered an Endangered species in Canada. Possible reasons for its decline include the loss of dead trees for nesting sites, competition with European Starlings for nest cavities, and the decline of American beech trees, whose nuts are an important food source. Call is a rolling, harsh *queeerk*.

Adult has all-red head. Body black above and white below. Large white wing patches.

Juvenile has brown head. Body brownish black above and whitish below. Underparts faintly streaked. White wing patches with some bands.

Red-bellied Woodpecker

Pic à tête rouge

Melanerpes erythrocephalus

L 23–24 CM (9 IN) | **WS** 33–42 CM (13–17 IN)

Unlike the Red-headed Woodpecker, the Red-bellied Wood-pecker has become more common in Ontario in the last few decades. The Ontario Breeding Bird Atlas recorded increases of 250 percent between the 1980s and 2000s. It is likely that warming climatic trends, the prevalence of bird feeders, and the increase of mature forests have all helped the woodpecker's range expand. It might be the most dominant bird visiting your feeder, even displacing belligerent Blue Jays. Call is a rolling, harsh *queerk*, very similar to the Red-headed Woodpecker's call but louder and clearer.

Adult male has bright red cap and nape and creamy face and belly with reddish patch between legs (rarely seen). Back and wings barred with black and white. (White rump and white "wrist" patches seen in flight.)

Adult female similar but with red on nape only.

American Three-toed Woodpecker

Pic à dos rayé

Picoides dorsalis

L 21–23 CM (8–9 IN) | **WS** 37–39 CM (14–15 IN)

This is the hardest regularly occurring woodpecker in Ontario to find. It lives in the boreal forest, where it depends largely on dead and dying trees and often forages in forests after they have burned. Instead of using its beak to drill into trees like many other woodpeckers, it flakes off loose bark in search of the bark beetle and wood-boring beetle larvae underneath. If you find one, try to count the three toes it has on each foot! Call is a repeated clear *check*.

Male has black head with yellow crown patch, white line through face, and possibly thin white eye line. Upperparts black with white barring on back and wing tips. Throat and underparts white with black barring on flanks. Outer tail feathers white. Female similar but lacks yellow on head.

Black-backed Woodpecker

Pic à dos noir

Picoides arcticus

L 23 CM (9 IN) | **WS** 40–42 CM (16 IN)

Like the American Three-toed, the Black-backed Woodpecker
is a boreal species that has only three toes on each foot. It will
flake bark off trees when foraging but also drills into the wood
to find food. Of the two woodpeckers, the Black-backed is
easier to find, though still challenging. The Thunder Bay and
Rainy River areas are good places to look. In southern Ontario,
your best bet is Algonquin Provincial Park, where the woodpecker is one of the park's four specialty birds. (The others are
the Canada Jay, Boreal Chickadee, and Spruce Grouse.) The
Black-backed's call is a harsh, emphatic, repeated *tek!*

Male has black head, yellow
crown patch, and white line
through face. Upperparts
black. Throat and underparts
white with black barring on
flanks. Outer tail feathers
white. Female similar but
lacks yellow on head.

Downy Woodpecker

Pic mineur

Dryobates pubescens

L 14–17 CM (5–6 IN) | **WS** 25–30 CM (10–12 IN)

The Downy Woodpecker is the smallest woodpecker in North America and a regular on the list of Ontario's top-10 feeder birds. Capable of becoming quite tame, it can even be taught to accept food by hand. Downy Woodpeckers often join chickadees, nuthatches, Brown Creepers, and kinglets in winter foraging flocks. It has been shown that the woodpeckers use chickadees as sentinels and react to the chickadees' alarm calls when a predator appears. It has also been found that both chickadees and nuthatches take evasive action after hearing the Downy's alarm calls. The woodpecker's call is a high-pitched repeated *tik*. Also makes a descending rattle.

Male has black and white striped head with red patch on nape. Beak short in relation to head size. Upperparts black with white spots and white back. Tail black. White outer tail feathers sport black spots. Female similar but lacks red on nape.

Hairy Woodpecker

Pic chevelu

Dryobates villosus

L 18–26 CM (7–10 IN) | **WS** 33–41 CM (13–16 IN)

The Hairy Woodpecker and Downy Woodpecker present a perennial identification challenge because they look so similar. The Hairy is significantly bigger than the Downy, but if the birds are not viewed together it can be hard to judge their sizes. Watch for the Hairy's all-white outer tail feathers and longer beak. Also, look at the red patch on the back of the male's head. In Ontario birds, a variable thin black line divides it into two red spots. Call is an emphatic *teek!* Also makes an evenly pitched rattle.

Male has black and white striped head with red patch on nape. Beak long in relation to head size. Upperparts black with white spots and white back. Tail black. White outer tail feathers lack black spots. Female similar but lacks red on nape.

Yellow-bellied Sapsucker

Pic maculé

Sphyrapicus varius

L 18-22 CM (7-9 IN) | **WS** 34-40 CM (13-16 IN)

True to its name, the Yellow-bellied Sapsucker does suck sap, or at least it laps it up with its feathery-tipped tongue. To get to the sap, the bird uses its laterally compressed beak to carve small squarish holes, called wells, in the bark of a tree, often in neat lines. The holes fill with sap, which the woodpecker later devours, along with insects that are attracted to the sap. Sapsuckers are a so-called keystone species, meaning they provide important resources to other creatures. Their sap wells give early spring nourishment to warblers, tanagers, orioles, hummingbirds, squirrels, wasps, butterflies, and other animals. Call is a whiny, hawk-like *keeyah*. Drumming pattern is a distinctive uneven series of taps.

Male has black and white head with red forehead and red throat. Upperparts and underparts white with dense mottling and variable yellowish wash on breast. Wings black with white shoulder patches. (Female similar, but throat white, not red.) Juvenile mottled brownish with black wings and white shoulder patches. Faint stripes on head.

Northern Flicker

Pic flamboyant

Colaptes auratus

L 28–31 cm (11–12 in) | **WS** 42–51 cm (16–20 in)

Studying the Northern Flicker allows you to see a lot of different field marks on one bird. The male, for example, sports a black breast patch and moustache, dark belly spots, striking barring on the back, and a bright red nape patch. And you can often get a good look, because flickers are regularly found on the ground, where they feed on ants. They also make their presence known with a variety of calls, including the fast, repeated *kick-kick-kick-kick-kick*. Northern Flickers breed across the province but overwinter only in the far southern areas.

Male light brown with grey cap and nape, black moustache, red crescent on nape, black breast band, and black spots on underparts. Black barring on back. Undersides of wing and tail feathers yellow. Female similar but lacks moustache.

Pileated Woodpecker

Grand Pic

Dryocopus pileatus

L 40–49 CM (15–20 IN) | **WS** 66–75 CM (26–30 IN)

The Pileated Woodpecker is as large as a crow, but it can be surprisingly secretive. It uses its large strong beak to excavate not only rectangular feeding holes in trees infested with carpenter ants, carpeting the forest floor below with woodchips, but also nest holes, which are round. When abandoned by the woodpecker, the nest cavities become nesting and/or roosting sites for Buffle-heads, Wood Ducks, Hooded Mergansers, Eastern Screech-Owls, Northern Saw-whet Owls, flying squirrels, and other wildlife, showing the Pileated's important role in the forest ecosystem. Call is a prehistoric-sounding *cuk-cuk-cuk-cuk-cuk-cuk-cuk*, hollower and more echoing than the call of a Northern Flicker. Also makes a short, spaced-out cluck.

Very large. Male has fully red cap and crest and red moustache. Head black and white striped. Body mostly black with some white on sides. White "wrist" patch on upper wing. (All-white wing linings visible in flight.) Female has black forehead and lacks red in moustache. Otherwise similar to male.

Peregrine Falcon

Faucon pèlerin

Falco peregrinus

L 36–49 CM (14–19 IN) | **WS** 100–110 CM (39–43 IN)

The Peregrine Falcon is the fastest animal on earth. When diving, it can reach speeds over 320 km/h (200 mph). Once endangered in North America, it has now returned to former cliffside nest sites and is even nesting on skyscrapers in many cities, all due to reintroduction efforts and the banning of certain chemical pesticides. Its recovery offers hope that other imperilled species have a chance if we put money and effort into saving them and their habitats. Peregrine Falcons migrate through Ontario regularly and spend the summer at nesting sites that are usually in cities or close to large bodies of water. Some may stay the winter in southern areas. Call is a loud *kak-kak-kak-kak-kak-kak*.

Flight very strong and fluid. Uses rowing motion when flapping and holds long, very pointed wings flat when soaring. Adult has black moustache and white throat and breast. Belly, undertail coverts, and wing linings white with dark barring. Tail long and grey with narrow dark bands.

American Kestrel

Crécerelle d'Amérique

Falco sparverius

L 22-31 CM (8-12 IN) | **WS** 51-61 CM (20-24 IN)

The American Kestrel is one of the most beautiful raptors on the planet. Decked out in blue, rufous, white, and black plumage, the male is pretty flashy, while the female is intricately barred above and streaked below. Since the kestrel is a cavity nester, a well-made nest box placed in open habitat that the falcons frequent in summer could attract a pair. American Kestrel numbers have dropped in recent decades in Ontario, as have numbers of many other grassland bird species. Call is a *killy-killy-killy-killy-killy*.

Male has rufous back with dark barring, pointed bluish-gray wings with dark spots, and long, bright rufous tail with thick black band near tip. Outer tail feathers white with dark spots. Face and throat white with thick black moustache and sideburns. Often hovers. Pumps tail when perched. Female (left) has barred rufous back, wings, and tail and more subdued head pattern with grey cap.

Merlin

Faucon émerillon

Falco columbarius

L 24–30 CM (9–12 IN) | **WS** 53–68 CM (21–28 IN)

While similar in size to the American Kestrel, the much more powerful Merlin is reminiscent of a tiny Peregrine Falcon. But Merlins do not make spectacular dives, as Peregrines do. Rather, they employ direct flapping attacks to chase down unwitting small birds that fly across open fields, beaches, or lakes. While kestrel numbers in Ontario have dropped in recent decades, Merlins have become more common, especially in cities, where they now nest in tall conifers in local parks or suburbs. Call is a *kek-kek-kek-kek-kek-kek-kek-kek*.

Adult male has bluish-grey head and upperparts, indistinct dusky moustache, and pale rufous to whitish underparts with dark streaks. Tail has thick black bands and thin white bands. Very strong flyer. Pointed wings. Tail has thick dark bands and thin white bands.

Gyrfalcon

Faucon gerfaut
Falco rusticolus

L 48–64 CM (19–25 IN) | **WS** 123 CM (48–49 IN)

The Gyrfalcon, the world's largest falcon, is one of the most sought-after birds in Ontario, if not all of Canada. It breeds on Arctic tundra and occurs in three main colours—grey, dark brown, and white—and all three morphs can occur in the province during migration or winter, or both. The best place to look for one is along the lakeshore in Thunder Bay, but the falcon also shows up in other locations in southern Ontario; the Ottawa area is often a good place to search. Any Gyrfalcon seen in the province is a rare treat. Call is a *kak-kak-kak-kak-kak-kak-kak*.

Grey-morph falcon has grey head with white throat, grey back and wings with faint barring, and white underparts with grey barring. Tail grey with narrow bands.

Long pointed wings but rounder tips than other falcons. Long tail. Strong flight. White-morph bird has all-white head, body, and tail with dark grey spots on back and wings and black wing tips. May have some dark barring on belly. Tail white with narrow dark bands.

Dark-morph falcon has dark brown head with lighter throat, dark brown body and wings, and dark brown underparts with whitish streaks or mottling. Tail brown with narrow dark bands

Western Kingbird

Tyran de l'Ouest

Tyrannus verticalis

L 20–24 cm (8–10 in) | **WS** 37–40 cm (14–16 in)

As the name suggests, this flycatcher is most often found to the west of Ontario, but it does show up annually and may even breed in the Rainy River area. Large and flashy with a beautiful yellow belly, it prefers open areas with good hunting perches, from which it sallies out to catch aerial insects or dives down for six-legged prey on the ground. Song is a chattering series of *pick* notes ending with a sharp *peek-a-boo!*

Not at all like Eastern Kingbird. Has light grey head and breast, whitish throat, hint of a dark mask, yellow belly, and black tail with white outer edges.

Eastern Kingbird

Tyran tritri

Tyrannus tyrannus

L 19-23 CM (7-9 IN) | **WS** 33-38 CM (13-15 IN)

This flycatcher is not shy about letting you know that you might be too close to its nest. Its alarm calls are noisy, and its fluttery flights above intruders are conspicuous. Any potential predator moving through its territory will be confronted. Many birders have seen a kingbird bravely peck at the head of a flying Red-tailed Hawk. Eastern Kingbirds are common in open areas over much of the province in spring and summer months. Song is a jumble of chattering, very high-pitched tick notes and buzzy *zeeee* notes.

Black head with white throat, dark grey upperparts, and white underparts. Orange crown spot usually concealed. Tail dark with white tip.

Great Crested Flycatcher

Tyran huppé

Myiarchus crinitus

L 17-21 CM (7-8 IN) | **WS** 34 CM (13 IN)

The Great Crested Flycatcher is our only flycatcher that nests in old woodpecker holes, tree cavities, or nest boxes. And when it builds a nest, it may include a shed snakeskin. The jury is still out on why the bird does this. One study showed that the presence of a snakeskin deterred flying squirrels from entering the cavity and reduced predation by small mammals. If a snakeskin is unavailable, the flycatcher may use a piece of clear plastic, such as a candy wrapper, that might be mistaken for the shed skin. Sounds include a loud *weep!* and a rolling, harsher *berrrt!*

Head and back greyish brown, belly and undertail coverts yellow, wings and tail rufous. Crest may be flattened or raised.

Eastern Phoebe

Moucherolle phébi

Sayornis phoebe

L 14–17 cm (5–7 in) | **WS** 26–28 cm (10–11 in)

The Eastern Phoebe often nests on the outside walls of house,
barns, and sheds. All it needs is a ledge of some sort with a roof
over it. It constructs its nest out of moss and mud and lines it
with grasses and hair. The Eastern Phoebe is double-brooded,
meaning it will nest a second time after the first brood's young
are independent, and it will reuse its own nest or, with a little
refurbishment, the old nest of a Barn Swallow or an American
Robin. Watch for the phoebe's bobbing tail to help distinguish it
from other flycatchers. Song is a continuous repeated *phee-bee!*
The second note is harsher and lower pitched than the first.

Dark greyish brown above
and whitish below with
variable yellowish wash
on belly and indistinct
wing bars. Lacks eye ring.

Olive-sided Flycatcher

Moucherolle à côtés olive

Contopus cooperi

L 18-20 CM (7-8 IN) | **WS** 33 CM (13 IN)

Larger than most of our greenish flycatchers, the Olive-sided Flycatcher is a bird of the coniferous forest but likes edges beside bogs, burns, and water, where it perches in the open and flies out to catch its aerial insect prey. It sings one of the more popular songs of any North American bird: *"Quick, three beers!"* Unfortunately, the flycatcher has declined since the 1980s and is now a species of special concern. It breeds in central to northern Ontario but can be seen in southern Ontario during migration.

Upperparts dark olive, underparts whitish with olive along sides. Lacks distinct wing bars. (May show white patches on sides of rump that can look like wing patches.) Spots on undertail coverts.

Eastern Wood-Pewee

Pioui de l'Est

Contopus virens

L 15 CM (6 IN) │ **WS** 23–26 CM (9–10 IN)

Pee-a-wee! Pee-yer! This loud, frequent, and easy-to-learn song will likely be your first clue that a forest contains at least one Eastern Wood-Pewee. The bird is a common denizen of wooded areas in southern Ontario, but finding its nest is challenging, as it is placed on a high horizontal branch and decorated with lichens to help it blend in. The wood-pewee has a weak or hard-to-see eye ring and long pointed wings whose tips extend well past the stacked secondary feathers when the wings are folded; these features help distinguish it from flycatchers in the genus *Empidonax*.

Olive-brown upperparts and dirty white underparts. Distinct wing bars and indistinct broken eye ring. Indistinct spots on undertail coverts.

Yellow-bellied Flycatcher

Moucherolle à ventre jaune

Empidonax flaviventris

L 13-15 CM (5-6 IN) | **WS** 18-20 CM (7-8 IN)

If you spot an Empidonax flycatcher with very green upperparts and yellow underparts, there is a good chance you
have found a Yellow-bellied Flycatcher. To be sure, listen for
its dropping song, *che-bunk*, or pewee-like call, *tu-whee*.
Even seasoned birders have trouble identifying Empidonax
flycatchers by sight alone. Recognizing their songs and calls is
the best way to confirm what you see. The Yellow-bellied nests
from Algonquin Provincial Park and scattered locations in
southeastern Ontario north to the Hudson Bay Lowlands.

Olive upperparts and
yellowish-olive
underparts. White eye
ring. White wing bars.

Acadian Flycatcher

Moucherolle vert

Empidonax virescens

L 14–15 cm (5–6 in) | **WS** 22–23 cm (9 in)

The rarest of Ontario's five Empidonax flycatchers, the Acadian Flycatcher was designated as Endangered in 1994. The province's population has stabilized but includes only 25–75 breeding pairs. Because the species is much more common in the eastern United States, its core range, efforts to save Ontario's flycatchers might be considered unwarranted, but species in the northern parts of their ranges are more adapted to shorter summers than those in the south. These adaptations are important to the species as a whole, making edge populations worthy of our protection. Listen for the rising *peeta-weet!* or falling *peet-zah*.

Olive upperparts and whitish underparts with slight yellow wash. Thin white eye ring and white wing bars.

Alder Flycatcher & Willow Flycatcher

Moucherolle des aulnes/Moucherolle des saules

Empidonax alnorum/Empidonax traillii

L 13-17 CM (5-7 IN) | **WS** 19-24 (7-10 IN)

The Alder Flycatcher and the Willow Flycatcher look so similar that they were considered the same species, known as "Traill's Flycatcher," until 1973. They can't be told apart easily by sight, so you must rely on your ears. The Willow Flycatcher sings a harsh *fitz-bew,* and its call is a bubbly *whit.* In contrast, the Alder Flycatcher sings a harsh *fee-bee-o, a*nd its call is a subdued *bip.* Because the song of some individuals is similar to that of the other species, however, you sometimes have to accept defeat and call a bird a "Traill's Flycatcher."

Alder (pictured) has olive upperparts, whitish underparts (may have slight yellow wash), thin white eye ring, and white wing bars.

Least Flycatcher

Moucherolle tchébec

Empidonax minimus

L 12–14 cm (5 in) | **WS** 20 cm (8 in)

The smallest of Ontario's five confusing Empidonax flycatchers, the Least Flycatcher is found in forested areas, where its emphatic *che-beck!* issues from the canopy. (Note the great onomatopoeic French name.) Curiously, Least Flycatchers can be common in one part of a forest and then not present in what seems (to us) to be the same habitat in another part of the same forest, and they often nest in clusters of other Least Flycatchers. Scientists have yet to figure out how this social aspect of the bird's life works. The flycatcher breeds across the province.

Largish head with white eye ring and white wing bars. Upperparts olive, underparts whitish (may have slight yellow wash).

White-eyed Vireo
Viréo aux yeux blancs
Vireo griseus

L 11–13 CM (4–5 IN) | **WS** 17 CM (7 IN)

Confined to breeding in the southernmost parts of the province, the White-eyed Vireo is always a target species for birders visiting places such as Point Pelee National Park or Rondeau Provincial Park. The vireo is usually found in scrubby thickets, where seeing it can be tricky. But like other vireos, it seems to have trouble keeping its mouth shut, so its whiny, chattering song will likely grab your attention. Listen for a variable catbird-like jumble of notes preceded and/or ending with a sharp *spit!*

Small, with grey head and greenish cap, back, wings, and rump, yellow "spectacles," and white iris. Beak strong compared to similar-looking warblers or kinglets. Wing bars white underparts whitish, flanks yellowish.

Red-eyed Vireo

Viréo aux yeux rouges

Vireo olivaceus

L 12–13 CM (5 IN) | **WS** 23–25 CM (9–10 IN)

The male Red-eyed Vireo whistles his song, remembered as *"Going up, coming down,"* more than any other eastern North American songbird—up to 20,000 times a day. He sings so much that during breeding bird surveys, which are often done by sound rather than sight, researchers have to be careful not to forget to listen for the species; the songs are so ubiquitous that surveyors can forget to count it. Red-eyed Vireos are found from the southern tip of the province to parts of the Hudson Bay Lowlands. Pauses between phrases sung by Red-eyed Vireos are usually shorter than pauses taken by similar-sounding vireos.

Large, with grey cap and black lateral crown stripe, white eyebrow, black eye line, and red iris. Upperparts olive green, underparts white. No wingbars. Beak strong compared to similar-looking warblers or kinglets.

Yellow-throated Vireo

Viréo à gorge jaune
Vireo flavifrons

L 13–15 CM (5–6 IN) | **WS** 23 CM (9 IN)

The Yellow-throated Vireo is found in deciduous and mixed forests in southern Ontario, especially in the Carolinian zone and in a band from Georgian Bay to Kingston. A bright yellow throat distinguishes it from other vireos, but caution is warranted because it does look surprisingly like many warblers, especially the Pine Warbler. Watch for the Yellow-throated Vireo's yellow "spectacles." If you get a good view, look also for a little hook at the end of its beak, which distinguishes vireos from warblers. Listen for a song that sounds like the repeated conversational double-notes of the Red-eyed Vireo or Blue-headed Vireo but with a hoarse or rough quality.

Stocky, with olive-green cap and back, yellow "spectacles," yellow throat and breast, and grey back and rump. Wing bars, belly, and undertail coverts white. Beak strong compared to similar-looking warblers or kinglets.

Blue-headed Vireo

Viréo à tête bleue

Vireo solitarius

L 12–15 CM (5–6 IN) | **WS** 22–24 CM (9 IN)

The Blue-headed Vireo sports a pair of white "spectacles," not yellow, as on the Yellow-throated Vireo. If you watch vireos in fall, you might see an interesting biological phenomenon: a major diet change. Vireos eat insects all spring and summer but add berries to their diet when they prepare to migrate. The antioxidants in the fruit help with the stress of migration, and the fat is deposited to fuel the long journey. The Blue-headed Vireo sings a series of conversational double notes slower than the Red-eyed Vireo.

Chunky, with bluish-grey head, white "spectacles," green back and rump, white wing bars and underparts, and yellowish flanks. Beak strong compared to similar-looking warblers or kinglets.

Philadelphia Vireo

Viréo de Philadelphie

Vireo philadelphicus

L 11–13 CM (4–5 IN) | **WS** 19–21 CM (7–8 IN)

This vireo has trouble getting noticed. It looks similar to the more common (in the south, anyway) Warbling Vireo, it sounds similar to a Red-eyed Vireo, and it breeds largely in the boreal forest, away from most birders. These points make seeing one a thrill. Be sure to look at the lores, the feathers between the eye and bill; they are darker on the Philadelphia Vireo than on the Warbling Vireo. And listen for the Philadelphia's song, which is slower and less bubbly than most Red-eyed Vireos' songs. For most Ontario birders, migration is the best time to see a Philadelphia. Get to know the more common Warbling Vireo well, so you don't overlook it.

Greyish olive above, with indistinct white eyebrow, indistinct dark eye line, and variable yellowish throat, breast, and undertail coverts. Seems bigger headed than Warbling Vireos. Beak strong compared to similar-looking warblers or kinglets.

Warbling Vireo

Viréo mélodieux

Vireo gilvus

L 12–13 CM (5 IN) | **WS** 22 CM (9 IN)

The Warbling Vireo may be drab, but it warbles better than most warblers, and its cheerful song will help you find it among the leaves of trees and shrubs in open woodlands, along river edges, and in hedgerows. Listen for this phrasing: *"If I sees you, I will seize you, then I'll squeeze you 'til you squirt!"* The male sings frequently throughout the day and will sing even while sitting on the nest. The Warbling Vireo breeds across southern Ontario.

Very dull. Olive-grey above and whitish below with indistinct white eyebrow. Slight eye line usually does not extend to beak. Flanks have variable amounts of yellowish wash.

Loggerhead Shrike
Pie-grièche migratrice
Lanius ludovicianus

L 20–23 CM (8–9 IN) | **WS** 28–32 CM (11–13 IN)

Also known as "butcherbirds," shrikes are songbirds that take a raptorial outlook on life. They catch small birds, mammals, and insects with their strong beaks and hang them on thorns to help rip off swallowable pieces. Shrikes may store leftovers on the same thorns or in crotches of trees. The Loggerhead Shrike is found across much of the United States; at the northern extent of its range in Ontario, it has become rare and is now considered Endangered. The best place to try to see one is the Carden Alvar, but only in spring and summer, as the bird leaves the province for the winter. Its call is a very harsh, jay-like scream.

Big headed, with grey upperparts, very light grey underparts, whitish throat, black mask, and hooked beak. Wings black with white patches. Tail black with white corners.

Northern Shrike

Pie-grièche boréale

Lanius borealis

L 23-24 CM (9 IN) | **WS** 30-35 CM (12-14 IN)

As its name suggests, this bird is from the far north. The Northern Shrike breeds in the Hudson Bay Lowlands in various open, woodland, and shrubby habitats. In winter, it spends its time across southern Ontario. Watch for it sitting on powerlines along farm fields or trying to grab a cardinal or junco in a backyard. Small birds know that this hunting songbird is trouble; their mobbing calls can alert you to its presence in your neighbourhood. Northern Shrikes are also found in eastern Asia. Calls are often harsh, jay-like screams.

Very similar to Loggerhead but larger and with smaller black mask. Both species may occur in southern Ontario in April. (First-winter shrike has indistinct mask and may have brownish wash.)

Canada Jay

Mésangeai du Canada

Perisoreus canadensis

L 25–33 CM (10–13 IN) | **WS** 45 CM (18 IN)

Destined to be the national bird, the Canada Jay embodies what many Canadians hope they represent: intelligence/resourcefulness (it stores food all fall so it can survive the winter and spring), toughness in all weather (it starts nesting in late winter, when snow often covers incubating females), and friendliness (it will readily land on your hand or picnic table for a peanut). Sadly, its range is retracting northwards. Temperature fluctuations due to climate change are causing its food caches to spoil in southern areas, thus decreasing the number of nestlings that survive. Listen for quiet whistles and harsh jay-like notes.

Adult looks like giant chickadee, with dark cap and white forehead, cheek, and nape. Beak short compared to other jays. Upperparts dark grey, underparts light grey. Tail feathers have white tips. Juvenile dark grey with light grey moustache.

Blue Jay

Geai bleu

Cyanocitta cristata

L 25-30 CM (10-12 IN) | **WS** 34-43 CM (13-17 IN)

The Blue Jay is one of our most popular birds, and not just because it is common at feeders or because a professional base-ball team is named after it, but because of its vivid colour. But unlike goldfinch feathers, whose brilliant yellow derives from a pigment, Blue Jay feathers lack blue pigment. The jay's colouration (like the colouration of all blue birds) is structural, the product of nanostructures on the feather surface that reflect blue light while absorbing all other colours. So, in low light, the jay looks not very blue, but in bright light, wow! Listen for the well-known harsh *jay!* call and a variety of other sounds. Blue Jays also mimic raptor calls.

Striking, with blue upperparts, whitish underparts, white eyebrow, and black eye line and collar. Wings and tail marked with black bars and white spots. Can flatten crest.

American Crow

Corneille d'Amérique

Corvus brachyrhynchos

L 40-53 CM (16-21 IN) | **WS** 85-100 CM (33-40 IN)

The commonly seen American Crow uses its intelligence and social prowess to survive in habitats ranging from remote forest to busy cityscapes. Telling a crow from a Common Raven can be a challenge. In flight, the crow shows a more rounded tail, spreads its wing tips more like fingers, and makes flappier wingbeats. It also has a smaller beak and smoother throat than its larger cousin. The Fish Crow, which is similar in appearance to the American Crow, has recently become more common in Ontario. Listen to a recording of its nasal *caa-aa* call to tell it apart from the American Crow's *caa*.

Large and all black with strong beak. Shows purplish sheen in some light. In flight, watch for round tail, spread finger-like wing tips, and flappy wingbeats.

Common Raven
Grand Corbeau
Corvus corax

L 56–69 CM (22–27 IN) | **WS** 116–118 CM (45–47 IN)

Brains, brawn, and bravado all come together with the Common Raven. Studies suggest it ranks as high as the chimpanzee in intelligence tests. It is also the largest songbird in the world. And it performs barrel rolls, flies upside down, steals food from wolves, and slides down snowbanks, apparently for fun. It used to be a bird of the north but recently has been expanding into southern parts of the province and using both rural and city landscapes. It can be garrulous and produces a complex array of vocalizations, including caws, rattles, knocks, and other sounds.

Very large (Red-tailed Hawk size) and all black with purplish sheen in some lights, very large beak, and shaggy throat feathers. In flight, note longer and more pointed wings than American Crow and wedge-shaped tail. Soars more and flaps less than crow.

Black-billed Magpie

Pie d'Amérique

Pica hudsonia

L 45-60 CM (18-24 IN) | **WS** 56-61 CM (22-24 IN)

This boldly marked member of the crow and jay family is restricted to extreme western Ontario, where it breeds in and around Dryden, Kenora, and Rainy River. There are a few southern Ontario records, but at least some of these sightings might be of birds that escaped from captivity. The Black-billed Magpie may take up to three months to construct its domed nest, and it often uses sticks bearing thorns, likely to give eggs and young extra protection from predators. Call is a repeated, nasal, up-slurred *yaaaaank*.

Large, with black head, breast, undertail coverts, and upperparts, white shoulders and belly, green/blue/purple iridescence in wings, and long tail. Large white patches in primaries visible in flight.

Tufted Titmouse

Mésange bicolore
Baeolophus bicolor

L 14-16 cm (5-6 in) | **WS** 20-26 cm (9-10 in)

A Tufted Titmouse would make a welcome addition to any bird feeder. Ontario is at the northern edge of the species' range. Finding one can be tricky unless you visit a southern forest, such as at Pinery Provincial Park, Rondeau Provincial Park, and the Dufferin Islands parking area just above Niagara Falls. The titmouse often forages in mixed flocks that may include chickadees, nuthatches, woodpeckers, and kinglets. Listen to a recording so you know what to listen for. The Tufted Titmouse's song is a whistled *peter, peter, peter, peter!*

Grey crest and black forehead. Upperparts grey, underparts white. Flanks orange.

Black-capped Chickadee

Mésange à tête noire

Poecile atricapillus

L 12–15 CM (5–6 IN) | **WS** 16–21 CM (6–8 IN)

So cute and so brainy, the Black-capped Chickadee has a memory that is hard to beat. It survives the winter by storing up to 1,000 seeds a day in fall. Then, not only does it remember where the seeds are hidden, but it knows which are richest in nutrients and which were eaten by another animal before it could get to them. The part of a bird's brain called the hippocampus is important for spatial memory. The hippocampus of a chickadee is larger than that of non-caching species, and studies have shown that its hippocampus is larger in fall than other times of the year — bigger when the bird needs it most. Makes many calls, but the best-known is *chick-a-dee-dee-dee-dee.* Whistles a clear song that sounds like *"Cheese bur-ger,"* with the second part lower in pitch than the first.

Large headed with short beak. White cheek separates black cap and throat. Upperparts grey, underparts white with buffy flanks and white edging on tail and wing feathers.

Boreal Chickadee

Mésange à tête brune

Poecile hudsonicus

L 12–14 cm (4–5 in) | **WS** 21 cm (8 in)

The best way to locate this sought-after shyer cousin of the
Black-capped Chickadee is to find a flock of Black-capped
Chickadees in fall or winter and listen. Try to hear the bird
that sounds harsher and more nasal. Then search the flock for a
brown-capped version of the other birds. Algonquin Provincial
Park is often the first place where southern birders will see a
Boreal Chickadee, but it can also be found in Thunder Bay and
Sault Ste. Marie, as well as in the depths of the boreal forest.
Call is a harsh, nasally *chick-dee*.

Large headed with short beak,
brown cap, and dark brown
throat. White cheek blends to
grey. Upperparts grey, underparts
whitish with buffy-orange flanks.

Bank Swallow

Hirondelle de rivage

Riparia riparia

L 12-14 CM (5-6 IN) | **WS** 25-29 CM (10-12 IN)

Considering its small feet and short legs, it is surprising how well this little guy can dig. Possessing bigger muscles that are associated with digging than other swallows, it can excavate burrows that are sometimes over 150 cm (5 ft) deep. It uses its conical beak to scrape at the soil during burrow construction as well. The male does the majority of the digging, while the female does most of the work on the nest, using grasses, rootlets, feathers, and leaves. Bank Swallows nest in colonies on vertical banks of rivers and in the walls of human-made gravel and sand pits. Call is a series of harsh, rough, short *chets*.

Small with brown upperparts, white throat and underparts, and brown breast band. In flight, note distinct breast band on white underparts. Tail forked.

Northern Rough-winged Swallow

Hirondelle à ailes hérissées

Stelgidopteryx serripennis

L 12-15 CM (5-6 IN) | **WS** 25-29 CM (10-12 IN)

Similar to the Bank Swallow but bigger and lacking a breast band, the Northern Rough-winged Swallow likes to place its nest in a burrow that already exists. This means it often uses the old burrows of Bank Swallows and Belted Kingfishers, as well as openings and crevices in bridges, culverts, gutters, and drainpipes. These human-made nest sites have likely helped the species expand its range, as it was uncommon in Ontario before the middle of the 20th century. The swallow's common name comes from a file-like edge on the male's first primary feather. The purpose of the adaptation is unknown. Call is a series of short, trilly, rolling *brits*.

Upperparts brown, underparts whitish with greyish-brown throat. Short tail lacks fork or has shallow notch.

In flight, note absent breast band and greyish-brown throat.

Tree Swallow

Hirondelle bicolore

Tachycineta bicolor

L 12-15 CM (5-6 IN) | **WS** 30-35 CM (11-14 IN)

The Tree Swallow is a so-called secondary cavity nester: it does not make its own cavity but uses a natural hole or the abandoned nest of a woodpecker (a primary cavity nester). Then the swallow actively defends its nest site. Because there usually aren't enough suitable cavities for all the birds looking for them, the resource can limit breeding. This is why bird box programs are important: they provide nest sites for the Tree Swallow and other secondary cavity nesters. The Tree Swallow is found across Ontario but is much more abundant in the southern part of the province. Call is a rapid, rich chirping.

Adult male shiny greenish blue above and bright white below. Female slightly duller, sometimes brownish. (Juvenile brownish.) Tail has shallow fork.

In flight, note shallow fork in tail (hard to see when spread) and bright white underparts.

Purple Martin

Hirondelle noire

Progne subis

L 19-20 CM (7-8 IN) | **WS** 39-41 CM (15-16 IN)

All bird houses are important, but for the Purple Martin, the human-bird association is critically important. In fact, in eastern North America, martins nest in bird houses and hollow gourds almost exclusively. The houses often have multiple rooms, each with its own entrance, to attract many pairs at once. Indigenous peoples started the practice, hanging gourds centuries ago. Martin numbers have plummeted across Ontario in recent decades, and many houses, once noisy with spring and summer activity, have fallen silent. Call is a down-slurred *tew*.

Male very large and dark. In bright light, note purplish-blue shine. Tail notched.

Female dark above and dirty white below with brownish throat. Tail notched.

Barn Swallow

Hirondelle rustique

Hirundo rustica

L 15–19 CM (6–7 IN) | **WS** 29–32 CM (11–13 IN)

A habit of nesting in barns, on light fixtures over front doors, and under porch eaves has made the Barn Swallow one of our most beloved birds. Unfortunately, like so many other birds that eat flying insects, it is declining. To think that the species would eventually be listed as Threatened in Canada would have been laughable 40 years ago. Let's hope that global environmental protection measures can happen quickly enough to allow it to become common again. Call is a staccato *leave-it*.

Upperparts black with bluish sheen. Forehead and throat rusty. Breast, belly and undertail coverts vary from orange to almost white. Tail forked with white spots. In flight, note deeply forked tail and rufous throat.

Cliff Swallow

Hirondelle à front blanc
Petrochelidon pyrrhonotas

L 13 CM (5 IN) | **WS** 28-30 CM (11-12 IN)

Hailing from cliff ledges of the West, the Cliff Swallow is a relatively recent addition to the avifauna of eastern North America. It nests under bridges, culverts, and roof overhangs, placing its intricate, gourd-shaped mud nest where a vertical wall meets a horizontal ceiling. The swallow constructs its nest out of mud pellets, which it brings to the site in its beak, taking about 24 hours to complete a nest. Cliff Swallows are found across southern Ontario, and there are colonies in the boreal region as well, though they are patchy and uncommon. Call is a series of burry notes.

Compact, with dark upperparts, whitish underparts, white forehead, light orange collar and rump, and dark rusty throat. Light streaks on back, grey smudges on undertail coverts. Orange rump and collar and white forehead stand out in flight.

Ruby-crowned Kinglet

Roitelet à couronne rubis

Corthylio calendulass

L 9–11 CM (3–5 IN) | **WS** 16–18 CM (6–7 IN)

The Ruby-crowned Kinglet is slightly larger than its golden-crowned cousin and not often found in Ontario in winter, but the male makes his spring return known with a loud and complex song. While he sings, he also performs a display in which he comically puffs up his crown feathers, revealing a tiny, usually hidden patch of red. The resulting punk hairdo is definitely worth focusing your binoculars on. His song starts with a few thin high-pitched notes, then jumps abruptly into a jumble of bubbly and musical phrases. Ruby-crowned Kinglets breed from southern Georgian Bay to the Hudson Bay Lowlands.

Larger headed than similar-looking warblers, with very small beak and broken white eye ring. Olive-grey above and grey below with bold white wing bar and yellowish edges to wing and tail feathers. Male has red crown (not always visible).

Golden-crowned Kinglet

Roitelet à couronne dorée

Regulus satrapa

L 8-11 cm (3-5 in) | **WS** 13-18 cm (5-7 in)

Except for the Ruby-throated Hummingbird, this is Ontario's smallest bird, yet it endures temperatures in northern areas that fall to –40°C (–40°F) in winter. How is this possible? At 5.7 g (0.2 oz), the Golden-crowned Kinglet is half the weight of a Black-capped Chickadee, and kinglets don't store food for the winter, as chickadees do. The kinglet survives because insulative feathers make up over 7 percent of its body weight and because it feeds constantly each day on tiny overwintering caterpillars that it finds hidden in tree branches. Call is a high-pitched, buzzy *zee-zee-zee.*

Like Ruby-crowned, but male has black-bordered yellow crown with orange center patch. (Orange patch can be concealed.) Female similar but without orange in crown.

Bohemian Waxwing

Jaseur boréal

Bombycilla garrulus

L 16–19 CM (6–8 IN) | **WS** 33 CM (13 IN)

Usually your first experience with a Bohemian Waxwing is noticing an extra-large member of a winter flock of Cedar Waxwings. A closer look reveals the Bohemian's chestnut undertail coverts, grey belly, and more colourful wing pattern, and if you listen, the Bohemian's trill is much harsher and lower than the Cedar Waxwing's. Bohemian Waxwings breed in the Hudson Bay Lowlands and the northern part of the boreal forest. In winter, they range widely, sometimes in flocks of over a hundred, looking for berry-producing woody plants. If the berries are in short supply in the north, the birds may show up in southern Ontario, delighting local wildlife photographers.

Striking, with long crest, grey underparts, chestnut undertail coverts, and wings tipped with black, white, red, and yellow. Head light greyish brown with thick black eye line and small black throat patch. Tail tipped with yellow.

Cedar Waxwing

Jaseur d'Amérique
Bombycilla cedrorum

L 14-17 CM (5-7 IN) | **WS** 22-30 CM (9-12 IN)

Even the most casual observers are struck by the Cedar
Waxwing's satiny plumage. The bird is named for the red tips of
the adult's secondary feathers. But the next time you see a flock
of waxwings, scan through it and check their tails. Fewer than
one in 100 Cedar Waxwings have at least one waxy tip on their
tails, and some waxwings get waxy tips on their primaries, too.
In the breeding season, watch for a charming courtship display
in which a male and female hop back and forth on a perch as
they pass a berry from one to the other and back again. Call is a
thin, high-pitched, slightly rough whistle.

Satiny, with brown head, breast, and
back, prominent crest, thick black eye
line, small black throat patch, and red
tips on secondaries. Rump and wings
grey. Belly yellowish. Undertail coverts
white. Tail grey with yellow tip.

Red-breasted Nuthatch

Sittelle à poitrine rousse

Sitta canadensis

L 11 CM (4 IN) | **WS** 18–20 CM (7–8 IN)

Nuthatches hunt for insects on tree trunks and branches by going any which way they want: up, sideways, or upside down. The Red-breasted Nuthatch prefers coniferous forests, while the White-breasted likes deciduous forests, but both birds are often found in mixed forests, where they may forage together with chickadees in winter. The Red-breasted Nuthatch is known to spread resin around the entrance hole of its nest cavity; it is thought that this deters predators and nest competitors. Call is a thin, nasally *yink*.

Adult male has black cap, white eyebrow, black eye line, and bicoloured, upturned, pointy beak. Throat white, underparts orange, and upperparts bluish grey. Tail short with white spots. Female similar but with dark grey cap and eye line. Usually less orange on underparts.

White-breasted Nuthatch

Sittelle à poitrine blanche

Sitta carolinensis

L 13–14 cm (5–6 in) | **WS** 20–27 cm (8–11 in)

The White-breasted Nuthatch is a common feeder visitor and can be trained to land on your hand for a peanut or sunflower seed. The bird may not eat the seed right away, though, as it caches food in fall and winter months. More than one person who has cut down a failing birch has been surprised to see the tree explode with sunflower seeds when it hits the ground: birch bark provides perfect storage crevices for an industrious nuthatch with access to a feeder. Call is a rough, nasal *yank! yank!*

Adult male has black cap, white face, white underparts, and pointy, upturned beak. Upperparts bluish grey. Rusty-orange patch on undertail coverts. Tail short with white spots. Female similar but has dark grey cap.

Brown Creeper

Grimpereau brun

Certhia americana

L 12-14 CM (4-6 IN) | **WS** 17-20 CM (7-8 IN)

A winter mixed flock of chickadees, nuthatches, and kinglets might include a tiny Brown Creeper as a member. The well-camouflaged bark explorer always spirals up a tree trunk. Relying on its stiff tail for support as it climbs, it uses its thin curved beak to grab any insect or spider hiding in the bark furrows. Once it gets high enough, it flies down to the bottom of another tree trunk and starts climbing again. Brown Creepers are found across the province but only in areas with forests containing fairly large trees. Call is a single high-pitched *seeeeeee*.

Very small, with long, thin, curved beak, white eyebrow, bark-like brown upperparts with black and white markings, and white underparts. White wing stripe. Long stiff tail has pointed feather tips.

Blue-gray Gnatcatcher

Gobemoucheron gris-bleu

Polioptila caerulea

L 10–11 CM (4 IN) | **WS** 16 CM (6 IN)

A little bird with a lot of attitude, the Blue-gray Gnatcatcher breeds in scrubby open woods, swamps, and deciduous forests, where it makes its presence known with a confident, high, whiny call. You will probably find one by hearing it first. The species has likely benefitted from a warming climate, as its range has expanded northward across southern Ontario in recent decades. Breeding males can be distinguished from females by the male's unibrow-like black forehead, which the female lacks. Gnatcatchers construct a tiny nest of plant fibers held tight with spider and caterpillar silk and covered with lichens for camouflage.

Tiny, with bluish-grey upperparts, whitish underparts, and white eye ring. Long tail black with white outer feathers. Female and non-breeding male lack black eyebrows of breeding male.

House Wren

Troglodyte familier

Troglodytes aedon

L 11-13 CM (4-5 IN) | **WS** 15 CM (6 IN)

The House Wren is a nondescript little brown bird with a big personality. It is easily attracted to most backyards with a well-made bird house. Instead of making just one nest, the male constructs many, filling all available cavities and crevices in the area with sticks. The female then chooses one and adds to the sticks a softer and more compact nest, where she will lay her eggs. It is thought that the unused nests, called dummy nests, may either show how fit the male is or dissuade predators, which presumably would give up after searching a few unused nests. The wren's song is a bubbly, musical series of trills and chatters.

All brown, lighter on underparts, with slightly curved, pointy beak, indistinct light eyebrow, and fine barring on wings, undertail coverts, and tail. Can hold long tail upright.

Winter Wren

Troglodyte des forêts

Troglodytes hiemalis

L 8-12 CM (3-5 IN) | **WS** 12-16 CM (5-6 IN)

Even smaller than the House Wren, the little Winter Wren has one of the longest songs of any North American bird: it can sing for up to 10 seconds. And it has been calculated that per unit weight, it sings 10 times as loud as a crowing rooster. Found in dense woods, the wren lives up to its name by remaining in parts of southern Ontario during the winter months. The best way to know if one is present is to listen for the chattering and belligerent call it makes when its territory is disturbed. It breeds in deciduous forests of the south but is more abundant in areas with conifers stretching from Algonquin Provincial Park to the boreal forest. Song is a very long series of fast, high-pitched musical trills that keep changing pitch.

Tiny and all dark brown, lighter on underparts, with pointy beak, light eyebrow, and fine black barring on wings, undertail coverts, and tail. Often holds short tail upright.

Sedge Wren

Troglodyte à bec court

Cistothorus stellaris

L 10–12 CM (4–5 IN) | **WS** 12–14 CM (5–6 IN)

The Sedge Wren likes to nest in tall sedges and grasses in wet or dry areas but can also be found in sphagnum bogs and hayfields. Very nomadic, it breeds in one place for a few years and then moves to another. Immature males don't copy the songs of other males that they hear when they are young (as many other birds do); they make up their own distinctive song types to use when breeding. Their variable songs usually consist of a few short, dry *teks* preceding a dry insect-like trill. Sedge Wrens are distributed patchily across southern and northwestern Ontario. "Sedge Wren Marsh" on Wylie Road in the Carden Alvar is one good place to look in spring and early summer.

Tiny, with buffy head and underparts, dark cap with fine light streaks, buffy eyebrow, and white throat. Back dark with thin white streaks. Rump cinnamon. Wings and tail barred.

Marsh Wren

Troglodyte des marais

Cistothorus palustris

L 10-14 CM (4-6 IN) | **WS** 17 CM (7 IN)

Unlike the Sedge Wren, the young male Marsh Wren learns its songs by copying the song types it hears other males sing. It can learn at least 200 song types this way. It uses the song fragments to battle other males for territory in the cattail marshes where it breeds. Marsh and Sedge Wrens can be tricky to tell apart visually. Watch for the Marsh Wren's rufous rump and shoulders and larger size. Marsh Wrens are found in suitable marshes in southern and northwestern Ontario. Their song is a variable series of tinkling, bubbling, and/or chattering trills.

Small, with longer beak than Sedge Wren and white eyebrow and throat. Upperparts reddish chestnut, especially on shoulders and rump. Back dark with thin white streaks. Underparts light with rufous wash. Dark bars on wings and tail.

Carolina Wren

Troglodyte de Caroline

Thryothorus ludovicianus

L 12–14 cm (5–6 in) | **WS** 29 cm (11 in)

The main range of the Carolina Wren in Ontario is the Carolinian forest, in the southern part of the province, but the wren has expanded northwards in recent years to spots such as Ottawa. This may be linked to warmer climatic conditions. The Carolina Wren does not migrate. When a pair shows up and breeds in a new place, the birds may remain there all year long. Even though this is our largest wren, it can be challenging to pick out from its often dense or tangled forest surroundings. It sings a rich, clear, distinctive song that sounds like *"Teakettle, teakettle, teakettle, teakettle!"*

Plump, with bright white eyebrow, brown upperparts, and white throat. Underparts bright buffy. Dark barring on wings, undertail coverts, and tail.

Horned Lark

Alouette hausse-col

Eremophila alpestris

L 16–20 CM (6–8 IN) | **WS** 30–34 CM (12–14 IN)

The tinkling song of a Horned Lark in late winter is a welcome sound that suggests spring is not too far away. The male often flies while singing. He climbs to a height of 80–250 m (260–820 ft), faces the wind, and then hovers in one spot, and he might sing in that spot for up to eight minutes. Horned Larks like areas with open bare ground and are found most often in cultivated fields. In late winter, they sometimes travel with flocks of Snow Buntings, so watch for darker birds among the lighter ones. Because Horned Larks prefer open areas, they breed in two discrete parts of Ontario: southern agricultural areas and the far northern edges of the Hudson Bay Lowlands.

Adult male has black mask, "horns," and breast patch, yellow throat, brown upperparts, and white underparts. Tail dark with white outer feathers. (Female duller and lacks "horns.")

Gray Catbird

Moqueur chat

Dumetella carolinensis

L 21-24 CM (8-10 IN) | **WS** 22-30 CM (9-12 IN)

Mee-aaah! It's not hard to figure out how the Gray Catbird got its name. Its nasal cat-like call is usually the first indication that one is concealed in a dense shrub. Its song is another clue: a jumble of many notes, whistles, and chatters interspersed with mew calls. The catbird's all-dark grey plumage and chestnut undertail coverts are distinctive, provided one finally pops out, so you can get a good look. Most of Ontario's Gray Catbirds are found in southern areas where clearing for agriculture and urban sprawl has led to the shrubby and garden areas they prefer.

Grey, with dark cap and chestnut undertail coverts. Tail and beak long.

Brown Thrasher

Moqueur roux

Toxostoma rufum

L 23–30 CM (9–12 IN) | **WS** 29–32 CM (11–13 IN)

Rich brown above and white below, with distinct dark breast spots, the Brown Thrasher looks like someone grabbed a Wood Thrush and gave it a good stretch, lengthening its tail and beak. An accomplished singer, the thrasher repeats its song phrases two times, distinguishing it from the less musical Gray Catbird and the more musical Northern Mockingbird. The Brown Thrasher is the only regularly occurring thrasher in eastern North America. It breeds across southern Ontario and ranges farther north where there is suitable shrubby habitat.

Large, with reddish-brown upperparts, white wing bars, white underparts, yellow eye, and long beak. Dark spots form long streaks on breast and belly. Tail very long.

Northern Mockingbird

Moqueur polyglotte

Mimus polyglottos

L 21–26 CM (8–10 IN) | **WS** 31–35 CM (12–14 IN)

Three members of the Mimidae, the family including mock-
ingbirds, thrashers, and the Gray Catbird, breed in Ontario. Of
these, the Northern Mockingbird is the champion mimic. The
male may incorporate the vocalizations of more than 10 bird
species into one bout of singing, intermingled with various
chirps, whines, and whistles, and the bird is known to sing at
night, especially close to the full moon. While common in the
United States, the mockingbird first bred in Ontario in 1906
and is now distributed patchily across southern areas. The
Niagara Peninsula and the west shore of Lake Ontario are good
places to look for it.

Slender, with grey upperparts, white
wing bars, dark eye line, and yellowish
eye. Underparts light grey. Tail long
with white outer feathers. Large white
wing patch visible in flight.

European Starling

Étourneau sansonnet

Sturnus vulgaris

L 20-23 CM (8-9 IN) | **WS** 31-40 CM (12-16 IN)

Even if you don't like the invasive nature of the European Starling, you have to admire its grit. Although only 100 birds were introduced in New York in 1890–91, more than 200 million starlings were estimated to be thriving all across North America one hundred years later. Their abundance makes them ideal for behaviour watching. For example, observe how they forage for invertebrates: they push their beak into the soil and then pry it open to look for a meal. European Starlings are accomplished mimics whose songs may include other birds' sounds.

Breeding adult all black with purple and green iridescence and pointy yellow beak. Wings and tail edged with brown. (Non-breeding bird covered in white spots and has dark beak.)

Juvenile brown with light throat and pointy dark beak.

Veery

Grive fauve
Catharus fuscescens

L 17–18 CM (6–7 IN) | **WS** 28–29 CM (11–12 IN)

Sporting a buffy breast with only muted spots, the Veery is our easiest *Catharus* thrush to identify. Its song is reminiscent of the sound you get when spinning a hose above your head: an airy spiralling whistle. It descends in pitch, whereas the song of the similar-sounding Swainson's Thrush rises in pitch. Because the Veery prefers secondary growth with an understory filled with shrubs and herbaceous plants, it benefits from logging. It breeds across most of southern Ontario and in the boreal forest.

Uniform light brown above with plain face. Whitish below with buffy breast and some muted brown spots. Greyish wash on flanks.

Gray-cheeked Thrush

Grive à joues grises

Catharus minimus

L 16-17 CM (6-7 IN) | **WS** 32-34 CM (12-13 IN)

Of Ontario's breeding *Catharus* thrushes, the Gray-cheeked is the hardest to see and the least abundant. Very few nests have been found in the province. The thrush migrates through southern Ontario to breeding grounds in the Hudson Bay Lowlands but is rather secretive. On its breeding territory, it is still hard to find even when listening for it—which is very odd, as other thrushes are loud and vocal. The Gray-cheeked Thrush sings a beautiful, though sometimes quiet, descending, airy song similar to that of the Veery but with gaps and starting with a couple short notes.

Uniform greyish-brown upperparts, plain greyish face, and broken white eye ring. Underparts whitish with grey wash on flanks. Dark spotting on breast.

Swainson's Thrush

Grive à dos olive
Catharus ustulatus

L 16-19 cm (6-8 in) | **WS** 29-31 cm (11-12 in)

Good field marks for the Swainson's Thrush, often described as the thrush with "spectacles," are a buffy eye ring and buffy feathers between the eye and beak. The bird is well known as a ground forager but regularly feeds higher in trees and shrubs than most of the other spotted thrushes in Ontario, and it also takes insects out of the air after flying out from a perch. It breeds from the Lake Simcoe area north to the treeline and is Ontario's most abundant *Catharus* thrush. Its population is estimated to be 8,000,000. Song is a rising, airy series of soft notes.

Rich olive-brown upperparts and flanks and prominent buffy "spectacles." Underparts whitish with dark spotting.

Hermit Thrush

Grive solitaire

Catharus guttatus

L 14–18 cm (5–7 in) | **WS** 25–29 cm (10–12 in)

One of the most beautiful in the avian world, the song of the Hermit Thrush has earned it nicknames such as "swamp angel" and "nightingale of (North) America." Visually, the bird stands out from the other spotted thrushes because of its reddish tail, which contrasts with its browner back. The Hermit Thrush breeds in habitats ranging from coniferous to deciduous forest and from tamarack bogs to recent burns. Its song consists of one or two airy whistles followed by multi-toned, descending notes that sound like a distant fairy's flute ensemble.

Olive-brown upperparts and flanks, reddish tail, and complete eye ring. Underparts whitish with dark spotting on the breast.

Wood Thrush

Grive des bois

Hylocichla mustelina

L 19-21 CM (7-8 IN) | **WS** 30-34 CM (12- 13 IN)

The Wood Thrush is the best-known spotted thrush for several reasons: Its uniform bright reddish-brown back and distinctly spotted white breast make it easy to identify. (Take care, though, not to confuse it with the larger Brown Thrasher.) It nests farther south than the other *Catharus* thrushes, so it can be found not only in local forests but also in wooded backyards throughout southern Ontario. And there is no lovelier addition to any warm summer evening than its beautiful fluted song: *yee-o-lay-yeeeeeee.*

Uniform reddish-brown upperparts, greyish face with white eye ring, and white underparts with distinct dark spots on breast and flanks.

American Robin

Merle d'Amérique

Turdus migratorius

L 20-28 cm (8-11 in) | **WS** 31-40 cm (12-16 in)

The American Robin is one of the first bird species we recognize. Its search for earthworms on a neighbourhood lawn is likely the first foraging behaviour we notice. And a robin's nest may be the first bird nest we ever see. Who isn't wowed by the robin's blue eggs? Many consider seeing the bird a first sign of spring, but robins overwinter in southern Ontario in large numbers and so can be seen throughout the year. They occur throughout the province but are most abundant in the south.

Adult male has dark grey head and back, rusty-orange breast and belly, yellow beak, and white patches around eye. (Female similar, but colours muted.) Juvenile greyish brown above with variable dark spots on orange-washed breast. Pale patches on face.

Eastern Bluebird

Merlebleu de l'Est

Sialia sialis

L 16–21 CM (6–8 IN) | **WS** 25–32 CM (10–13 IN)

By putting out thousands of nest boxes along roadsides and field edges, dedicated volunteers helped the Eastern Bluebird recover from a decline in the 1970s that had caused the species to be designated Rare. By 1996 it was delisted. The easiest way to find a bluebird today is to drive a country road in spring or summer and watch for boxes on fence posts. Some Eastern Bluebirds overwinter in Ontario; seeing one feeding on berries in a snowy landscape is a cold-weather treat. Song is a chattery series of soft flutelike whistles. Call is a soft, musical *too-e-you*.

Male has brilliant blue upperparts, orange throat, breast, and flanks, and white belly and undertail coverts.

Female similar, but colours muted. Head and back feathers more greyish blue. Throat whitish.

House Sparrow

Moineau domestique

Passer domesticus

L 14-16 CM (5-6 IN) | **WS** 19-25 CM (7-10 IN)

A successful introduced species, the House Sparrow is one suave city slicker. It has learned to warm itself beside street-lights. It steals food from restaurants. It even flies in front of motion detectors to open shopping-mall doors. Unfortunately, it can also be destructive, outcompeting native chickadees, bluebirds, and swallows for nest cavities. House Sparrows were first noted in Ontario around 1870 and subsequently spread across southern Ontario and into a few northern areas. Recently, though, their numbers have been dropping for reasons that are not completely understood. Makes a series of loud chirps.

Male in summer has grey crown, black face, chin, and breast, and black beak. Upperparts rich brown. Back streaked, with white wing bar and greyish-white cheek, sides, belly, and undertail coverts. In winter, male duller with less black on face, breast, and beak.

Female has greyish-brown head and body, buffy eyebrow, indistinct eye line, and pale beak. Back streaked with thin wing bar. Breast plain greyish brown.

American Pipit

Pipit d'Amérique

Anthus rubescens

L 14-17 cm (5-7 in) | **WS** 25-28 cm (10-11 in)

The American Pipit migrates through much of Ontario but nests in the Hudson Bay Lowlands, close to the coast. It also breeds across the Arctic as well as in western North America and Asia. When it is passing through southern Ontario, look for it in open farm fields and along shorelines, including inland lakes. It lacks the "horns," mask, and chest patch of the similar Horned Lark, and its beak is thinner than a streaky sparrow's beak. Call is a high-pitched *wit*.

More like small thrush than sparrow, with thin beak, thin eye ring, and pale eyebrow and throat. Upperparts brown with white wing bars. Underparts white to creamy with dark streaks on breast. Outer tail feathers white.

Evening Grosbeak

Gros-bec errant

Coccothraustes vespertinus

L 16–18 CM (7–8 IN) | **WS** 30–36 CM (12–15 IN)

The spectacular Evening Grosbeak showed up as a provincial breeder in the early 1920s and by the 1980s was fairly common and sometimes abundant at winter feeders. The increase was likely due to spruce budworm outbreaks. When they decreased, grosbeak numbers dropped, too, and the species is now listed as Special Concern. When an irruption occurs in southern Ontario, everyone with a feeder stocks up on sunflower seeds and eagerly waits for the finches to come and eat. Some northern communities get grosbeaks throughout the winter; birders travel from southern Ontario to Algonquin Provincial Park to observe them at the visitor centre. Calls are a series of chirps similar to those made by the House Sparrow.

Male has dark brown head with yellow eyebrows and forehead and large pale beak. Large white wing patch. Lower back and belly yellow.

Female has large beak, grey head and body, and grey and white patches on black wings.

House Finch

Roselin familier

Haemorhous mexicanus

L 13-14 CM (5-6 IN) | **WS** 20-25 CM (8-10 IN)

The House Finch is native to western North America but was once sold in pet stores in the East. A shop owner in New York released some of the so-called Hollywood finches in 1940 (to avoid being fined for selling a native species), and the birds started to breed and spread. Because western populations are also expanding, the finch will soon be found across the continent. It arrived in Ontario in 1972 and is now common in suburbs, where it visits feeders and builds its nest in conifers, hanging flower baskets, and decorative door wreathes. Song is a musical but raspy warble.

Male has red forehead, eyebrow, breast, and rump, brown upperparts with streaks on back, brown streaks on breast, sides, and undertail coverts, and thin wing bars. Orange or yellow replaces red on some individuals.

Female and first-year male have brown head and upperparts, streaked back, dirty white underparts, brown streaks on breast and sides, and thin wing bars.

Purple Finch

Roselin pourpré

Haemorhous purpureus

L 12–16 CM (5–6 IN) | **WS** 22–26 CM (9–10 IN)

To tell Purple Finches from House Finches, compare eyebrows, underparts, and colouration. Female Purple Finches have white eyebrows and very white underparts with dark streaks. Female House Finches lack eyebrows, and their underparts are dirty white with blurry streaks. Male Purple Finches look like they were dipped in raspberry juice (they really should be named "raspberry finches"), while the orangish-red colouration of male House Finches tends to be concentrated on their forehead, breast, and rump. The Purple Finch's song is a rich, fast, slightly hoarse warble.

Male has raspberry-red head, breast, sides, and rump, reddish wash on back and wings, brown streaks on back, and indistinct (or absent) brown streaks on flanks. Belly and undertail coverts white. Wing bars reddish. Sometimes shows small crest.

Female and first-year male have white eyebrow and throat, brown, streaky upperparts, and white underparts with dark streaks on throat, breast, and sides. Thin white wing bars. Sometimes shows small crest.

Pine Grosbeak

Durbec des sapins
Pinicola enucleator

L 20-25 CM (8-10 IN) | **WS** 33-35 CM (13-14 IN)

Pine Grosbeaks breed in the boreal forest and Hudson Bay
Lowlands but are so secretive that they can be hard to observe.
When they come south in winter, birders celebrate. Like the
Bohemian Waxwing, another northern species, the Pine Gros-
beak depends on berries for sustenance, though it tends to
focus on the seeds inside the berries rather than the fruit pulp.
Finding a winter flock of Pine Grosbeaks on a native mountain
ash or a roadside ornamental crabapple is always thrilling.
Calls are clear rich whistles.

Male has bright
raspberry-red head,
breast, sides, and
rump, short black
eye line, streaked
back, white wing
bars, and grey belly.

Female similar but
grey and lacks red.
Head and rump
olive or yellowish.
Throat grey. Rusty
colour may replace
olive on first-year
male and some
females.

Pine Siskin

Tarin des pins

Spinus pinus

L 11–14 CM (4–6 IN) | **WS** 18–22 CM (7–9 IN)

In winter, an American Goldfinch that seems extra streaky is likely a Pine Siskin. It often shares nyjer feeders with goldfinches and redpolls, if they are around. Feisty and nomadic, the siskin will fly long distances across the continent to find its favourite conifer seeds. In areas with a good crop, it may start nesting as early as February. Its breeding distribution is patchy in southwestern Ontario but becomes more common northwards into the boreal forest. The siskin makes many jumbled, chattering notes and a rising raspy trill.

Tiny, with thin, pointy, conical beak, brown, streaky upperparts, and yellowish to white wing bar. (Yellow wing stripe visible in flight.) Underparts white with dark streaks on breast, sides, and undertail coverts. Yellow in tail.

American Goldfinch

Chardonneret jaune

Spinus tristis

L 11–13 CM (4–5 IN) │ **WS** 19–22 CM (7–9 IN)

Because the American Goldfinch is one of our most common backyard birds, the male's brilliant yellow, the female's lovely olive green, and the browns and whites of winter birds can all be enjoyed up close and personal. Goldfinches wait to nest much later in the season than other birds so they can take advantage of an abundance of weed seeds, which they feed to their nestlings. Most small birds give their young insects, from which the nestlings obtain the proper proteins for feather growth, but goldfinch nestlings do fine with only seeds. Song is a series of long warbling twitters and trills. Whistles a rising call sounding like *"Pot-a-to chip!"*

Male in summer has bright yellow head and body, black forehead, black wings and tail, and orange beak. Wing bar, rump, and undertail coverts white. Extensive white spots in tail.

Female has olive-green upperparts, yellowish underparts, and pink beak. Wings and tail dark brownish black with white or buffy wing bar. Undertail coverts white. Extensive white spots in tail.

In winter, similar to summer female but greyer. Wings and tail black or brownish black. Beak dusky. Less yellow on breast.

Common Redpoll

Sizerin flammé

Acanthis flammea

L 12–14 CM (5–6 IN) | **WS** 19–22 CM (7–9 IN)

The Common Redpoll usually appears in southern Ontario in winter only when spruce and birch crops farther north are low. The tiny pink-flushed bird has very dense feathers that help it stay warm in the coldest weather, and it is known to burrow into snow to take advantage of its insulating properties overnight. Common Redpolls breed in the Hudson Bay Lowlands and across the southern Arctic. Calls include a rising *teeeew* and variable harsh chips and trills.

Male has black face and chin, red cap, striped back, and white wing bars. Rump usually streaked. Underparts white. Variable pink wash on breast and rump and dark streaks on sides. Thin streaks on undertail coverts.

Female similar but lacks or has very little pink. More heavily streaked.

Hoary Redpoll

Sizerin blanchâtre

Acanthis hornemanni

L 12-14 cm (5-6 in) | **WS** 20-25 cm (8-10 in)

Along with the Lapland Longspur and Snow Bunting, the Hoary Redpoll is one of the most northerly breeding perching birds in the world. Nests found in Ontario along the coast of Hudson Bay are at the southernmost edge of its breeding range, which extends to the northern reaches of Ellesmere Island, in the Arctic. When wintering Hoary Redpolls occur in southern Ontario, they are found in flocks of Common Redpolls; watch for the Hoary's whiter rump and underparts as well as its stubbier beak. Both redpolls can be attracted to feeders filled with nyjer and sunflower seeds. Calls include variable harsh chips and trills.

Male has black face and chin and red cap. Stubby beak makes face look pushed in. Back streaked. Wing bars white. Usually no streaks on rump. Underparts white with light pink wash on breast and rump and very thin streaks on sides. Undertail coverts lacks streaks or have only a few thin streaks. Female similar but lacks pink. Heavier streaking.

Red Crossbill

Bec-croisé des sapins

Loxia curvirostra

L 14-20 CM (6-8 IN) | **WS** 25-27 CM (10-11 IN)

Recordings of flight calls have revealed that as many as 10 "call types" of the Red Crossbill exist across North America. Birds of different call types eat the seeds of specific conifer species, they have beak shapes and sizes that are best suited to extracting seeds from specific cones, and some are known to range widely in search of good cone crops. The variations between the types could eventually lead to the splitting of the Red Crossbill into different species. In Ontario, the Red Crossbill's main breeding range reaches from Algonquin Provincial Park to the boreal forest. Calls are a series of short, choppy, loud notes.

Male has crossed beak and dull red body. Dark wings and tail. (First-year male yellowish.)

Female has crossed beak and yellowish-olive or olive-grey body. Rump yellowish.

White-winged Crossbill

Bec-croisé bifascié

Loxia leucoptera

L 15-17 CM (6-7 IN) | **WS** 26-27 CM (10-11 IN)

Like the Red Crossbill, the White-winged Crossbill uses its funky beak to access conifer seeds. It sticks its beak tips between the scales of a cone and spreads them sideways, prying the scales apart. Then it reach in with its tongue to extract the seed. White-winged Crossbills whose lower mandible crosses to the right are three times more common than those whose lower mandible goes left. (The direction dictates which foot the bird usually uses to hold the cone.) Both crossbills may move south of their normal ranges in winter if cone crops up north fail. The White-winged's songs and calls are a series of short notes and mechanical trills.

Male has crossed beak, pink body, black wings and tail, and bold white wing bars. (First-year male orange or yellowish.)

Female has streaked brownish-grey body with variable yellowish wash on breast and rump and blurry streaks on breast. Wings and tail brownish. Bold white wing bars.

Lapland Longspur

Plectrophane lapon
Calcarius lapponicus

L 15–16 CM (6 IN) | **WS** 22–29 CM (9–11 IN)

One of the most northerly breeding birds in the world, the Lapland Longspur nests in the province only along the Hudson Bay coast. In southern Ontario, it can be found during winter and migration. In winter, your best strategy is to search through flocks of Snow Buntings for darker birds. If these aren't Horned Larks, they are likely Lapland Longspurs. In late winter and early spring, you might find a flock of migrating longspurs that contains males almost changed into their gorgeous breeding plumage. Call notes include a short, rough whistle.

Longspurs in winter have light brown head and dark-bordered cheek. Upperparts streaky brown, underparts whitish with variable amounts of dark streaks on breast and flanks. White wing bar. Chestnut patch on wing. (Breeding female similar but has more black on face and breast and chestnut on nape.)

Breeding male has black head. Wide white eyebrow goes down side of neck. Nape chestnut red. White wing bar. White underparts. Black streaks or patches on breast and flanks. Outer tail feathers white.

Snow Bunting

Plectrophane des neiges

Plectrophenax nivalis

L 15 CM (6 IN) | **WS** 30 CM (12 IN)

The Snow Bunting, an Arctic breeder, has been confirmed nesting in the province only once (in the Hudson Bay Lowlands), but that doesn't mean you won't get to see it. In winter, southern Ontario's open agricultural fields host hundreds of Snow Buntings. Interestingly, not all of the over-wintering birds go to the Canadian Arctic to breed; banding data shows that many fly to western and southern Greenland instead. Calls include a fast but short chattering trill and a short clear whistle.

In winter, bunting has whitish head and underparts and white wing patches. Brown wash on face, crown, and breast. Back streaky brown. (First-winter bird browner with less white in wings. Breeding male all white with black back and tail. Breeding female has greyer upperparts.)

Extensive white in wings and tail can make buntings flying over snow hard to see.

Chipping Sparrow

Bruant familier

Spizella passerina

L 13–15 CM (5–6 IN) | **WS** 19–21 CM (7–8 IN)

A suburban favourite, the tiny Chipping Sparrow likes to nest in the little spruce trees that dot the front lawns of so many new neighbourhoods. The female does the building, placing the nest between two overlapping branches. It usually takes four days to build. On Day 1, a pile of rootlets is formed. On Day 2, the rootlets are arranged into a donut shape. On Day 3, the donut is transformed into a cup with a bottom. And on Day 4, the nest is lined with hair. The sparrow once used horsehair for this, earning it the nickname "horsehair bird"; now it often incorporates dog fur and human hair instead. Song is a long dry trill.

Summer adult has rufous cap, white eyebrow, black eye line, and dark beak. Nape grey. Upperparts streaked brown with white wing bars and grey rump. Throat and undertail coverts white. Underparts light grey.

Winter adult similar but with brownish cap (may show some rufous), buffy eyebrow, brown eye line, and pinkish beak.

Clay-colored Sparrow

Bruant des plaines

Spizella pallida

L 13–15 CM (5–6 IN) | **WS** 18–20 CM (7–8 IN)

This sparrow is found more commonly out west, but it does breed in Ontario, and its numbers have been increasing for almost a decade. Its insect-like *bzzzz bzzzz bzzzz* is loud and memorable. Listen for it whenever you visit a grassy, brushy field, and especially if young conifers are scattered throughout. The male often sings close to where the female is sitting on a nest. The Clay-colored Sparrow's very patchy distribution in the province includes the south, the northwest, even the Hudson Bay Lowlands.

Summer adult has white eyebrow, buffy cheek patch with dark border, dark moustache, and grey nape. Wing bars white. Back brown and streaked, underparts grey. (Winter adult similar, but head markings less distinctive. Buffy wash on breast, sides, and eyebrow. First-winter sparrow may be buffier.)

Field Sparrow

Bruant des champs

Spizella pusilla

L 12–15 CM (5–6 IN) | **WS** 20 CM (8 IN)

The distinctive song of the Field Sparrow will help you identify it: imagine a Ping-Pong ball dropped on a table, bouncing faster and faster. That is the basic pattern of its slurred notes. The sparrow looks similar to other reddish-capped species, but note the bright all-pink beak. Only the bill of the immature White-crowned Sparrow, a much larger bird, is similar. Field Sparrows nest in old fields across southern Ontario, and most leave in winter, but some may still be found in the extreme southern areas.

Adult has grey head with rufous cap and eye line, pink beak, and white eye ring (sometimes hard to see). Brown streaky upperparts. Rump grey. White wing bars. Underparts greyish with variable rufous wash on sides

American Tree Sparrow

Bruant hudsonien

Spizelloides arborea

L 13–15 CM (5–6 IN) | **WS** 23–25 CM (9–10 IN)

Ontario birders observe this sparrow most often in winter as it hangs out at feeders or in weedy fields, sometimes with Dark-eyed Juncos. It looks so similar to the Chipping Sparrow that it was once classified in the same genus, but the species is now thought to be more closely related to the Fox Sparrow. Look for the American Tree Sparrow's rusty eye line and bicoloured beak, and don't be misled by its name. On the bird's sub-Arctic breeding grounds (which include the Hudson Bay Lowlands), it nests on or near the ground and often nowhere near substantial trees. Call is a high, musical *diddily*.

Rufous crown, grey head, rufous eye line, and bicoloured beak. Underparts greyish white, with central breast spot. White wing bars, streaked back, and faint rufous wash on sides.

Fox Sparrow

Bruant fauve

Passerella iliaca

L 15-19 CM (6-8 IN) | **WS** 26-29 CM (10-11 IN)

Fox-like rufous and grey plumage makes this one of our most striking sparrows. It is also one of our biggest sparrows and a treat to spy in a thicket or under a feeder during migration or in winter. The Fox Sparrow nests in Ontario in the northern boreal forest and the Hudson Bay Lowlands, where it proclaims its territory with a beautiful, whistled song that includes clear strong notes and ends in a phrase that sounds like *aujourd'hui!*

Relatively large, with grey head with rufous on crown and face, rufous streaked upperparts, thin white wing bars, and grey rump. Breast and belly white with rufous streaks on breast and sides. Can be confused with Hermit Thrush.

Dark-eyed Junco

Junco ardoisé

Junco hyemalis

L 14–16 CM (5–6 IN) | **WS** 18–25 CM (7–10 IN)

"Grey skies above and white snow below, is how you can tell that it's a junco." The easy-to-identify Dark-eyed Junco is the second most common winter feeder bird in Ontario. (The first is the Black-capped Chickadee.) Taxonomists organize the continent's many subspecies of junco into half a dozen groups. Members of the grey "Slate-colored" group occur in the province most often, but the rare hooded "Oregon" form shows up sometimes, too. Dark-eyed Juncos breed mostly from the Kawartha Lakes north to the Hudson Bay Lowlands. Song is a musical, tinkling trill on one pitch.

Adult male has dark grey upperparts, throat, breast, and sides, white belly and undertail coverts, and pink beak. Outer tail feathers white.

Adult female and first-year male similar but paler with variable brownish wash.

White-crowned Sparrow

Bruant à couronne blanche

Zonotrichia leucophrys

L 15–16 CM (6 IN) | **WS** 21–24 CM (8–9 IN)

The White-crowned Sparrow is striking because of its large size as well as its skunk-patterned head. It breeds in the province's far north, where the boreal forest blends into the Hudson Bay Lowlands. Most birders in southern Ontario see it during the spring and fall migrations. They remember its song, heard often in spring, with the fun phrase *"I gotta go wee wee now."* The White-throated Sparrow is one of the most studied birds on the planet and has helped us discover many details about songbird biology.

Adult has black crown with white central crown stripe, white eyebrow, black eye line, pink beak, and grey cheeks and neck. Brownish streaked back with a greyish-brown rump. Wing bars white. Breast grey. First-winter sparrow (right) similar, but head stripes brown, not black. Eyebrow and central crown stripe buffy. Cheeks buffy.

White-throated Sparrow

Bruant à gorge blanche

Zonotrichia albicollis

L 16–18 CM (6–7 IN) | **WS** 20–23 CM (8–9 IN)

The White-throated Sparrow occurs in two colour morphs: white-striped and tan-striped. Curiously, an individual of one colour almost always pairs up with a sparrow of the opposite colour, a system not shared by any other bird species. Since the white-striped sparrows are more aggressive/defensive and the tan-striped birds make better parents, pairing one with the other may be the best breeding strategy. Song is a high, whistled phrase that sounds like *"Home sweet Canada Canada Canada."*

Fairly large. White-striped adult has black crown and white central stripe with white eyebrow, black eye line, yellow between eye and beak, grey cheek, and white throat. Brown streaked back with brownish rump. Wing bars white. Breast grey.

Tan-striped adult similar, but head stripes dark brown with buffy central crown stripe. Eyebrow tan. Feathers between eye and beak dull yellow. Buffy wash on face and underparts. Some birds, especially in winter, have blurry breast streaks and possibly central breast spot.

Harris's Sparrow

Bruant à face noire

Zonotrichia querula

L 17-20 CM (7-8 IN) | **WS** 25-28 CM (10-11 IN)

The Harris's Sparrow is the only bird that breeds in Canada
and nowhere else. It has been recorded in Ontario along the
Hudson Bay coast a few times during the breeding season, but
only one nest (1983) has ever been found in the province. The
sparrow overwinters in the south-central United States but can
sometimes be seen in northwestern Ontario during migration.
As well, vagrants may show up at feeders in southern Ontario
during winter. Song is a series of two or three pure whistles,
similar to those made by the White-throated Sparrow but
mostly on one pitch.

Fairly large. Adult in summer has grey head
with black crown, face, throat, and upper
breast and pink beak. Brown streaked back,
thin white wing bars, and greyish-brown rump.
Breast greyish with black streaks on side.

Sparrow in winter similar but for buffy cheek
and eyebrow and less black on head.
First-winter sparrow (left) has white throat
bordered with black.

Vesper Sparrow

Bruant vespéral

Pooecetes gramineus

L 13–16 CM (5–6 IN) | **WS** 23–25 CM (9–10 IN)

The Vesper Sparrow can be tricky to identify because it looks so similar to the Song Sparrow and the Savannah Sparrow. Watch for the Vesper's slight eye ring and, when it flies, white outer tail feathers. With luck, you may also see its most distinctive field mark: a chestnut shoulder patch that once earned the bird the name "bay-winged bunting." The sparrow is a bird of open grasslands, and its numbers in Ontario have dropped in recent decades, likely because the agricultural areas it prefers are being managed more intensively than before. Song is similar to that of the Song Sparrow but more musical. It starts with two pairs of notes; Thoreau described it as *"Here here there there quick quick quick or I'm gone."*

Dark-bordered cheek patch and thin white eye ring. Streaked brown above with chestnut shoulder patch (often concealed). Fine dark streaks on white or buffy breast and sometimes central breast spot. Outer tail feathers white.

LeConte's Sparrow

Bruant de LeConte

Ammospiza leconteii

L 12–13 CM (5 IN) | **WS** 15–18 CM (6–7 IN)

"Sharp-tailed" sparrows are known for being secretive. Instead of flushing, they will often try to avoid being seen by running along the ground in their grassy habitats like little feathered mice. The LeConte's Sparrow is not particularly abundant anywhere in Ontario, even though it breeds across the province (though in small numbers in southern Ontario). Listen for singing males in wet meadows and sedge marshes in places such as Sault Ste. Marie, Rainy River, and Moosonee. Their song is a hissing, insect-like *tika-zzzzzzzzzz-tik*.

Small, with white central crown stripe, buffy yellow eyebrow and face, grey cheek, and grey nape with reddish streaks. Upperparts brown streaked. Breast buffy, with narrow dark streaks on breast and sides. Belly whitish. Tail feathers pointed.

Nelson's Sparrow

Bruant de Nelson

Ammospiza nelsoni

L 11–13 CM (4–5 IN) | **WS** 16–20 CM (6–8 IN)

The Nelson's Sparrow nests in Ontario at two main locations: one is the Hudson Bay Lowlands, and another is the Rainy River area, which is part of a population across Alberta, Saskatchewan, and Manitoba. These populations and another in the Maritime provinces make Canada the home to over 75 percent of the world population. During migration, Nelson's Sparrows can be found in wet grassy areas in southern Ontario, sometimes with similar-looking LeConte's Sparrows. If you are lucky enough to see a Nelson's, look at its nape, which is plain grey. On the LeConte's, it is grey with thin rusty lines. Song is a sizzling, hissy *puh-shhhhhhhhhhhhhh-tuk*.

Like LeConte's, but with bright buffy orange face and eyebrow, plain grey cheek and nape, and grey central crown stripe. Upperparts brown streaked. Breast bright buffy orange with blurry brown streaks on sides. Belly white. Tail feathers pointed.

Henslow's Sparrow

Bruant de Henslow

Centronyx henslowii

L 11-13 CM (4-5 IN) | **WS** 16-20 CM (6-8 IN)

Another casualty of intensive farming, the Henslow's Sparrow is Ontario's only Endangered sparrow species. It received this dreary provincial designation in 1993. Numbers of the rare, skulking bird have declined steadily since the 1980s, and it is now found breeding in Ontario at only a couple sites each year. Most of these records are of vocalizing males, which sing *tse-lick*. The song is so quiet and short that finding the sparrow is very challenging. Because of its secretive nature, it is one of North America's least-known sparrow species.

Very small, with large beak, olive green face, and buffy central crown stripe. Upperparts steaked with brown. Rufous in wings. Breast buffy with narrow dark streaks on breast and sides. Belly whitish. Tail feathers pointed.

Grasshopper Sparrow

Bruant sauterelle

Ammodramus savannarum

L 11-12 CM (4-5 IN) | **WS** 20 CM (8 IN)

This shy, elusive, little bird was once called the "yellow-winged sparrow" because of its hard-to-see tiny yellow patch on its shoulder. But "grasshopper" is a great name, too, because the sparrow's buzzy song is similar to the sound made by the insect. Knowing the song is crucial, since finding the bird is very difficult without hearing it first. Listen in dry, open grasslands that have rough terrain and some short shrubs. Song is a couple short, quiet chip notes followed by the insect-like buzz.

Small, with fairly large beak, flat head, and buffy face with thin whitish eye ring and dark spot behind eye. Orangish between eye and beak. Dark cap has whitish central crown stripe. Grey nape has thin rusty streaks. Yellow sometimes seen at bend of folded wing. Breast buffy, belly whitish, tail short.

Savannah Sparrow

Bruant des prés

Passerculus sandwichensis

L 11–15 CM (4–6 IN) | **WS** 20–22 CM (8–9 IN)

This sparrow is a common breeding bird in open grassland, meadow, and grazed areas. You may think that the name "Savannah" is linked to these treeless habitats, but the sparrow is named after Savannah, Georgia. It sings frequently. The thin buzzy notes of its song seem to say, *"Won't you come sit down besiiiiiiiiide meeeeeee?"* Yellowish lores, the feathers between the eye and beak, thin breast streaks, and a short tail help distinguish the sparrow from the similar-looking Song Sparrow. The Savannah Sparrow's breeding range in Ontario is split by the forested regions: it nests across southern Ontario and in the Hudson Bay Lowlands.

Variable, with white central crown stripe and often yellowish lores. Brown streaked above. Underparts white with fine dark breast streaks and often central breast spot. Tail shortish, notched.

Song Sparrow

Bruant chanteur

Melospiza melodia

L 12–17 CM (5–7 IN) | **WS** 18–24 CM (7–9 IN)

The adaptable Song Sparrow can be found in a wide range
of habitats: along river edges, on islands and shorelines of
lakes, along forest margins, in the shrubby edges of fields and
agricultural areas, and in backyards and city parks. It breeds
across the whole province but is more abundant in the southern
region. Most of Ontario's Song Sparrows depart for the winter,
but some stay and are often found in wet marshy areas along
rivers or wetlands. The sparrow sings a complex series of
whistles and trills that starts with a few similar short notes;
the song is often described as *"Madge Madge Madge put on the
teakettle kettle kettle kettle."*

Stocky, with brown-streaked upperparts, very
thin white wing bars, and white underparts
with thick brown streaks on breast and sides
and usually strong central breast spot.
Pumps long rounded tail in flight.

Lincoln's Sparrow

Bruant de Lincoln

Melospiza lincolnii

L 13-15 CM (5-6 IN) | **WS** 19-22 CM (8-9 IN)

Breast patterns can be species specific and thus helpful when identifying similar-looking sparrows. The pattern of the Lincoln's Sparrow is distinctive. It has thin dark streaks and a central spot on a buffy breast and flanks which contrast with its white throat and belly. The sparrow migrates through southern Ontario and nests mostly from the Algonquin Provincial Park area to the Hudson Bay Lowlands, where it is most abundant. The Lincoln's Sparrow is secretive and often on or near the ground, so it is a good idea to check every scurrying sparrow carefully during migration. Song is a series of fluid House Wren–like trills constantly changing in pitch.

Thick grey eyebrow and thin buffy eye ring. Brown streaked above. White throat. Buffy breast and sides covered in thin dark streaks. Often has small central breast spot. Belly white.

Swamp Sparrow

Bruant des marais

Melospiza georgiana

L 12-15 CM (5-6 IN) | **WS** 18-19 CM (7 IN)

Cattail marshes, shrubby swamps, and other wet areas with lots of cover attract the Swamp Sparrow. These habitats can make getting a good look challenging unless the bird in question is a male singing from an exposed perch. The sparrow often forages at the water's surface and will wade right in to grab a meal, even sticking its head fully underwater. Swamp Sparrows breed across the province wherever the proper habitat is found. Song is a long, slow, musical trill.

Adult in summer has reddish crown. Face and sides of neck grey with dusky eye line, white or whitish throat, and brown-streaked upperparts. Wings rufous. Breast grey. Sides buffy.

Adult in winter similar but with dark-streaked brown crown. Faint streaks on breast. Possible faint central breast spot. Buffy wash on cheeks.

Eastern Towhee

Tohi à flancs roux

Pipilo erythrophthalmus

L 17–21 CM (7–8 IN) | **WS** 20–28 CM (8–11 IN)

The Eastern Towhee forages by scratching its feet through leaves. The action is so noisy that many hikers and naturalists who have heard it have thought a bear or moose was close by. Once called the "Rufous-sided Towhee," the sparrow was split into the Eastern Towhee and the Spotted Towhee in 1995. The Eastern breeds across southern Ontario and sometimes spends the winter, while the Spotted sometimes occurs in winter as a vagrant, so any towhee seen in that season should be checked carefully for spots on the wings. Song is a ringing whistle sounding like *"Drink your teeeeea!"*

Male large with long tail, black head, breast, and upperparts, white belly, and rufous sides. Corners of tail white. Female (left) similar, but brown replaces black.

Yellow-breasted Chat

Ictérie polyglotte

Icteria virens

L 18 CM (7 IN) | **WS** 25 CM (10 IN)

The Yellow-breasted Chat has been a taxonomic challenge. The species was once placed in the family of New World warblers, but its large size and complex song never seemed to be a good fit. Now it is in its own family and thought to be most closely related to New World blackbirds. The Yellow-breasted Chat has decreased in Ontario and was listed as Endangered in 2011. It likes to use very dense brushy habitats and would be hard to find but for its loud, varied, chattery song, which is full of mews, whistles, and pure notes. Watch for it at spring migration hot spots, such as Point Pelee, Rondeau, and Long Point.

Large, with heavy beak, black feathers between eye and beak, white moustache, and yellow throat and breast. White eyebrow joins broken eye ring. Upperparts brownish olive. Belly and undertail coverts white. (Female similar but slightly paler with dark grey between eye and beak.)

Bobolink

Goglu des prés

Dolichonyx oryzivorus

L 15–21 CM (6–8 IN) | **WS** 26–28 CM (10–11 IN)

The male Bobolink often sings while making special display flights over its territory, and any fan of the movie Star Wars should enjoy the song, since it contains mechanical phrases similar to those made by the robot character R2-D2. The Bobolink is a bird of open fields, and it is declining, harmed by the loss of suitable breeding habitat following the intensification of agriculture and by the early harvesting of hayfields where it may nest. The bird breeds across southern and northwestern Ontario where suitable open habitat occurs. It was listed as Threatened in 2010.

Male in summer all black with yellow hindcrown and nape, whitish shoulders and rump, and short sparrow-like beak.

Female very sparrow-like, with thick buffy eyebrow, dark crown streaks, and dark line behind eye only. Nape unstreaked. Brown streaks on back and breast.

Eastern Meadowlark

Sturnelle des prés

Sturnella magna

L 19-26 CM (7-10 IN) | **WS** 35-40 CM (14-16 IN)

The Eastern Meadowlark is another open-area songbird that is declining. Though it can still be found in fields and meadows, it is listed as Threatened. The Western Meadowlark *(Sturnella neglecta)* is nearly identical, but the yellow on its throat is often more extensive. It usually occurs only in the northwestern part of the province but does show up as a rarity in southern Ontario as well. The two birds have very different songs: the Eastern whistles a thin, high-pitched tune that sounds like *"Sweet spring is here,"* while the Western makes a fluid, rich, descending warble.

Long, pointy, grey beak and pale face with dark crown stripes and eye line. Feathers between eye and beak and on throat, breast, and belly yellow. Flanks pale with dark streaks. Back mottled brown. Short tail has white outer feathers. Legs long and pink.

Orchard Oriole

Oriole des vergers

Icterus spurius

L 15-18 CM (6-7 IN) | **WS** 25 CM (10 IN)

The rusty-orange adult male Orchard Oriole is fairly easy to identify, but the first-year male, with a black face and yellow body, is sometimes mistaken for a kind of warbler. The oriole prefers scrubby habitats and open forest and was once rare in most of southern Ontario but has increased in number in areas with suitable habitat in recent decades. Where it had been restricted mostly to the Carolinian forest, it is now expanding north and east into the Great Lakes-Saint Lawrence forest region. Listen for a high-pitched squeaky warble.

Adult male has rusty-orange breast, belly, undertail coverts, rump, and shoulder, black head and upperparts, and white wing bar.

Female olive-yellow with indistinct eye line, dusky cap and upperparts, and two white wing bars. (First-year male similar but with black mask and throat.)

Baltimore Oriole

Oriole de Baltimore

Icterus galbula

L 17–19 CM (7–8 IN) | **WS** 23–30 CM (9–12 IN)

The Baltimore Oriole is much more common and widespread than the Orchard Oriole, and the male sports a dazzling combination of bright orange, black, and white that makes him easy to identify. What's more, the bird's simple whistled song is clear and recognizable. Baltimore Orioles in the northern part of their range in Ontario have decreased in recent decades, as natural succession has caused open areas to become more mature forests, which are not to this species' taste. The oriole weaves a bag-like nest at the tip of a drooping branch to protect against climbing predators.

Adult male has black head and upperparts, bright orange shoulder, breast, belly, undertail coverts, and rump, and white wing bar. Corners of tail orange.

Female and first-year male yellowish orange with variable (or absent) dusky markings on head, dusky back, and two white wing bars. Flanks pale.

Yellow-headed Blackbird

Carouge à tête jaune

Xanthocephalus xanthocephalus

L 21-26 CM (8-10 IN) | **WS** 42-44 CM (16-17 IN)

Yellow-headed Blackbirds defend nesting territories aggressively. They even chase away Red-winged Blackbirds, displacing them to other parts of the marsh. The Yellow-headed breeds only in the extreme northwestern and southwestern areas of the province. The male's bright yellow head, jet-black body, and white wing patches are striking, and he might sing the strangest song in Ontario: a harsh, mechanical, grinding sound.

Adult male has yellow hood, black mask, all-black body, and white wing patch.

Female has yellowish face and breast. Cap and body all brown.

Red-winged Blackbird

Carouge à épaulettes

Agelaius phoeniceus

L 17-23 CM (7-9 IN) | **WS** 31-40 CM (12-16 IN)

Abundant in summer in marshes, swamps, and other wetlands, the Red-winged Blackbird is well known—or at least the male is. The brown, sparrow-striped female is often overlooked, which is just what she wants. Since she is the one who does all of the incubation, blending in works best for her. Meanwhile, the male shows off his bright red epaulettes and sings his raspy *"Hercules!"* to warn rivals not to enter his patch. The blackbird nests across all of Ontario except for the northern parts of the Hudson Bay Lowlands.

Male all black. Red shoulders have yellow bar. (First-year male browner; some look similar to females.)

Female very sparrow-like but with larger, pointier beak. Eyebrow and throat buffy with dark eye line and moustache. Back streaked reddish brown with pale wing bars. Underparts whitish with dark streaks.

Brown-headed Cowbird

Vacher à tête brune

Molothrus ater

L 16–22 CM (6–9 IN) | **WS** 32–38 CM (13–15 IN)

Why raise your own young when someone else can do it for you? This is the MO of the Brown-headed Cowbird, a so-called nest parasite. But this doesn't mean the cowbird is lazy. The female, for instance, has to spend time finding other birds' nests to lay her eggs in. While most small birds lay four to eight eggs in a season, she lays an egg a day for 30–40 days. And many of those eggs will be rejected or abandoned by the host. The male cowbird sings a complex song of bubbly notes and high-pitched whistles, often while performing a display in which he spreads his wings and tips forward.

Male has brown head and shiny all-black body.

Female plain brown with lighter-coloured throat and plain face.

Common Grackle

Quiscale bronzé

Quiscalus quiscula

L 28-34 CM (11-13 IN) | **WS** 36-46 CM (14-18 IN)

Some people just don't like the resourceful Common Grackle, which travels in noisy flocks, dominates feeders, breeds almost everywhere in the province, and is all black with no markings. But the grackle deserves a second look: Its long pointy beak complements a long keeled tail, and that black plumage sets off bright yellow eyes. In the right light, the bird shimmers with beautiful blue, purple, green, and bronze iridescence. Plus, one of its many calls is a wacky *GLOINK!* made while fluffing its body feathers.

Slender, with long pointy beak, yellow eye, and all-black body. Purplish-blue iridescence on head and bronze iridescence on body. Tail very long and keeled.

Rusty Blackbird

Quiscale rouilleux

Euphagus carolinus

L 21-25 CM (8-10 IN) | **WS** 36-38 CM (14-15 IN)

It's nice when a bird has a descriptive name, as this blackbird does. Both the male and the female show rusty colouration in winter, and part of the male's song can sound like a rusty hinge on a metal gate. The blackbird has declined dramatically in recent times for reasons that aren't clear. Habitat loss and degradation and pesticide use may be playing a role. The Rusty Blackbird breeds in the southern Canadian Shield, boreal forest, and Hudson Bay Lowlands and spends the winter in the south-eastern United States. It was listed as Special Concern in 2006.

Male in summer all black with muted purplish-green iridescence, yellow eye, and slightly curved beak.

Female in winter has prominent buffy eyebrow and throat, yellow eye, rusty-brown cap, nape, and back, and greyish rump. Underparts buffy with rusty and grey mottling. (Female in summer more uniform greyish brown. Winter male similar, but body blacker and less buff.)

Brewer's Blackbird

Quiscale de Brewer

Euphagus cyanocephalus

L 20-25 CM (8-10 IN) | **WS** 36-38 CM (14-15 IN)

This western blackbird is usually found only in the Rainy River and Sault Ste. Marie areas and on the Bruce Peninsula. In summer, the male looks very similar to a male Rusty Blackbird, but the Brewer's has a thicker and pointier beak, its plumage is glossier, and its song is buzzier and less musical. The male Brewer's could also be confused with the Common Grackle, but note its square, unkeeled tail and smaller beak. The female Brewer's Blackbird usually has dark eyes, whereas the female Rusty has pale eyes.

Male in summer black with purplish-green iridescence, yellow eye, and pointy beak.

Female greyish brown, with dark eye. Beak pointier than on female Brown-headed Cowbird.

Ovenbird

Paruline couronnée

Seiurus aurocapilla

L 11–14 cm (4–6 in) | **WS** 19–26 cm (7–10 in)

"Teacher teacher teacher teacher!" Thank goodness that this otherwise secretive warbler has such an easy-to-learn and loud song to help identify it. If it weren't for the song, the bird's smaller size, and an orange stripe on the top of the head, the Ovenbird might be thought to be a miniature thrush. Unlike most other warblers, it does not hop as it forages on the forest floor; it walks. The bird was named after its well-camouflaged domed nest, which has a side opening, like an old-fashioned oven. Parents take care when walking to and from it to protect their nestlings and eggs. The Ovenbird breeds in forested areas across Ontario.

Handsome, with two black stripes on either side of orange crown, whitish eye ring, and white underparts with dark spots on breast and sides. Throat white with dark moustache. Back and rump olive brown. Legs pinkish. No tail spots.

Worm-eating Warbler

Paruline vermivore

Helmitheros vermivorum

L 11–13 cm (4–5 in) | **WS** 20–22 cm (8–9 in)

This is a tough-to-find warbler that rewards observers willing to wait patiently for it to pop out of a densely vegetated hiding spot. The Worm-eating Warbler has yet to be found breeding in Ontario but is sometimes seen in spring at migration hot spots such as Point Pelee National Park or Rondeau Provincial Park. Surprisingly, given its name, the warbler does not eat earthworms; it prefers caterpillars (which once were known as "worms"), other insects, and spiders, which it gleans from leaves. It also eats slugs. Song is a long dry trill.

Buffy head, dark eye line, and dark stripes on sides of crown. Upperparts olive green, underparts buffy. Legs pinkish.

Louisiana Waterthrush

Paruline hochequeue

Parkesia motacilla

L 15–16 CM (6 IN) | **WS** 23–28 CM (9–11 IN)

The Louisiana Waterthrush is a regular but local breeder in the Carolinian forest of southern Ontario and was listed as Threatened in 2015. It prefers wooded habitat near clear, cold, flowing streams. Along with the Ovenbird and the Connecticut Warbler, both the Louisiana Waterthrush and Northern Waterthrush are walkers, but the waterthrushes add another behavioural field mark: a constantly bobbing rear end, reminiscent of a Spotted Sandpiper. The Louisiana's song starts off with a few loud whistles, then changes to a scrambled mix of quieter twittering notes.

Like Northern, but white eyebrow (possibly grey or buffy near eye) does not grow noticeably thinner behind eye. Eye line and upperparts brown. Underparts white with dark streaks and often some buff on flanks. Legs usually bright pink.

Northern Waterthrush

Paruline des ruisseaux

Parkesia noveboracensis

L 12–14 cm (5–6 in) | **WS** 22–26 cm (9–10 in)

The Northern Waterthrush can be tricky to tell apart from the Louisiana Waterthrush. Watch for the Northern's duller legs, smaller beak, streaked throat, and thinner and tapering eyebrow. As well, some Northern Waterthrushes are yellowish below; the wash is not seen on the Louisiana Waterthrush. Common in wet woods and along river edges across the province, Northern Waterthrushes are most abundant in the Hudson Bay Lowlands and the northern parts of the boreal forest. Song is a loud three-part series of fluid notes: *weet weet weet weet wee wee wee chew chew chew.*

Like Louisiana but with light yellow, buffy, or white eyebrow that usually grows thinner behind eye. Eye line and upperparts brown. Underparts light yellow, buffy, or white with dark streaks. Throat often has dark spots. Legs dull pinkish.

Golden-winged Warbler

Paruline à ailes dorées

Vermivora chrysoptera

L 11–12 CM (4–5 IN) | **WS** 20 CM (8 IN)

The Golden-winged Warbler and Blue-winged Warbler have a special relationship: they hybridize where their ranges overlap. The resulting hybrids are called the "Brewster's" and "Lawrence's" warblers. The "Brewster's" hybrid generally lacks the Golden-winged's head pattern and is grey above and white below, while the "Lawrence's," the rarer of the two, displays the Golden-winged's black mask and the Blue-winged's yellow underparts. The hybrids are known to sing the song of either non-hybrid parent. The Golden-winged's song is a buzzy *bees buzz buzz buzz*. Under pressure from habitat loss and the expansion of the Blue-winged Warbler, the species has been listed as Threatened since 2006.

Male Golden-winged in spring has black throat and mask, white moustache, yellow crown, and white eyebrow, with grey back and rump and yellow wing patch. Breast, belly, and undertail coverts whitish. Tail spots white. (Female similar, but grey replaces black.)

Female "Lawrence's" variable but usually has grey mask and throat and yellowish head and underparts.

Blue-winged Warbler

Paruline à ailes bleues

Vermivora cyanoptera

L 11-12 cm (4-5 in) | **WS** 15 cm (6 in)

The Blue-winged Warbler is becoming more common in
Ontario, and the increase is coming at the expense of the
Golden-winged Warbler. As more Blue-wingeds move into
historic Golden-winged habitat, chances increase that the
species will hybridize, reducing the Golden-winged's overall
population size. Blue-wingeds need only about 50 years to take
over an area that was once occupied by Golden-wingeds only.
The preferred habitat in southern Ontario for both species is
early successional scrubby areas. The Blue-winged Warbler
sings a buzzy *bees buzzzzzz*.

Male in spring has all-yellow head with black eye line.
Back and rump olive green. Wings bluish grey with
white wing bars. Breast and belly yellow with white
undertail coverts. Tail spots white. (Female similar but
duller.)

"Brewster's" usually has grey upperparts and white
underparts. May have yellow throat or spot on breast.

Black-and-white Warbler

Paruline noir et blanc

Mniotilta varia

L 11–13 cm (4–5 in) | **WS** 18–22 cm (7–9 in)

The well-named Black-and-white Warbler is indeed a mono-chromatic blend of black and white stripes, but that doesn't mean it isn't striking. It stands out by how it searches for food on tree trunks: sideways, upwards, downwards, and upside down. This nuthatch-like foraging once earned the warbler the name "black-and-white creeper." You might think that such a manoeuvrable bird would build an arboreal nest, but no, it nests on the ground. The Black-and-white Warbler sings a thin *wheesy wheesy wheesy wheezy*, often described as a squeaky wheel.

Male in spring black and white striped with white eyebrow and moustache, black cheeks and throat, and black-and-white crown. Wing bars white. Large white tail spots. (First-spring male lacks or has less black in throat.)

Female similar but has white throat and plainer face with light grey cheeks. Thin black eye line starts behind eye. May have buffy flanks. Streaking on underparts less distinct.

Prothonotary Warbler

Paruline orangée
Protonotaria citrea

L 13 cm (5 in) | **WS** 21–23 cm (8–9 in)

The Endangered Prothonotary Warbler is a local nester in deciduous swamps of the Carolinian region of Ontario, which are at the northern edge of the species' overall range. The province's only cavity-nesting warbler, the Prothonotary relies largely on Downy Woodpeckers to provide nest holes but uses human-made nest boxes as well. The best place to see the warbler in Ontario is Rondeau Provincial Park, where it breeds consistently. Its song is a ringing *weet weet weet weet weet*.

Male in spring has golden head, breast, and belly, green back, and grey rump. Undertail coverts white. Wings bluish grey. White spots on tail.

Female in spring duller with greenish-yellow crown and nape.

Tennessee Warbler

Paruline obscure

Leiothlypis peregrina

L 10–13 CM (4–5 IN) | **WS** 18–20 CM (7–8 IN)

The Tennessee Warbler is one of Ontario's drabbest warbler species, making it a challenge to identify. The male makes up for his muted garb by singing a loud, distinctive, three-part trill similar to the two-part song of the Nashville Warbler. To remember which is which, note that the word Tennessee has three syllables while the word Nashville has two. The Tennessee Warbler breeds from Algonquin Provincial Park north to the Hudson Bay Lowlands. It specializes on eating spruce budworms during outbreaks.

Male in spring has grey head with white eyebrow and throat and dark eye line. Back and rump bright green. Underparts whitish, sometimes with light yellow wash on breast. White spots on tail.

Spring female and fall warbler similar but with greyish-green head. Yellowish eyebrow and throat and light yellow on breast and sides. Often no white spots on tail. Dusky eye line. Note whitish undertail coverts.

Orange-crowned Warbler

Paruline verdâtre

Leiothlypis celata

L 11-14 CM (4-6 IN) | **WS** 18-20 CM (7-8 IN)

You might think that looking for orange crown feathers would be a good plan for identifying an Orange-crowned Warbler, but you would be wrong. The little orange tuft is often covered up or even absent. You would be better off looking for a usually drab greenish bird whose yellow undertail coverts are its most noticeable feature. Also note its broken eye ring and faint eye line and breast streaks. Orange-crowned Warblers nest in the far north of Ontario, so most are seen only during migration. The warbler sings a quick trill that drops in pitch at the end.

In spring has short dusky eye line, faint narrow broken eye ring, and faint streaks on sides of breast. Orange crown may be concealed or absent. Throat dull whitish olive. Olive-green back a bit brighter at rump. Upperparts and underparts yellowish olive with brighter yellow undertail coverts. No tail spots.

Fall bird similar but greyer, especially on head of some individuals.

Nashville Warbler

Paruline à joues grises
Leiothlypis ruficapilla

L 11–13 cm (4–5 in) | **WS** 17–20 cm (7–8 in)

Like the Mourning Warbler and the Connecticut Warbler, the male Nashville Warbler is yellow below and green above and has a bluish-grey hood. Look for its yellow throat, which is lacking in the males of the other two species. The Nashville's underparts are also distinctive: all yellow except for some white around the legs. The warbler nests in a variety of habitats, from second-growth forests to open scrubby fields to bog edges. Listen for its two-part trill, the first part slower than the second.

Male has bluish-grey head, yellow throat, and white eye ring, as well as chestnut patch on crown. Back olive green. Rump greenish yellow. Breast yellow, belly whitish, and undertail coverts yellow. No tail spots.

Female similar but with brownish-grey head and little chestnut on crown. Underparts dull yellow.

Connecticut Warbler

Paruline à gorge grise

Oporornis agilis

L 13–15 cm (5–6 in) | **WS** 22–24 cm (9–10 in)

The Connecticut Warbler nests in the boreal forest and Hudson Bay Lowlands and migrates through southern Ontario, but it's so hard to see that it might be the last species you need to complete your provincial warbler list. Unlike most other warblers, it walks instead of hops, and it walks in such a controlled way that it seems to glide along the forest floor, making it difficult to pick out. Learning the warbler's song can be helpful: listen for *chuck chuck chuck chuckity chuckity chuck!* It sounds like a Common Yellowthroat that is having trouble getting its song started.

Male has bluish-grey hood and bold white eye ring. Upperparts olive green. Underparts yellow with some olive green on sides. Legs pink. No tail spots.

Female and first-winter bird similar but with brownish hood and buffy or whitish throat.

Mourning Warbler

Paruline triste

Geothlypis philadelphia

L 10–15 CM (4–6 IN) | **WS** 18 CM (7 IN)

Shy and tricky to spot, the Mourning Warbler spends much of its time on or near the ground in dense young growth in disturbed areas that are slowly growing back into forest. Adult males sport a black breast patch, as if dressed for mourning, but first-year males may be much duller and could lack black entirely. The warbler breeds from southern Ontario to the southern parts of the Hudson Bay Lowlands. Its song is a rich, two-part *cheery cheery cheery chorry chorry*, the last part lower in pitch and quieter than the first.

Adult male has olive upperparts, yellow underparts, bluish-grey hood, and variable dark patch on breast. Female similar but with light grey hood and no black on breast.

Kentucky Warbler

Paruline du Kentucky

Geothlypis formosa

L 13 cm (5 in) | **WS** 20–22 cm (8–9 in)

Though this warbler doesn't breed in Ontario, a few are found each spring. They are considered "overshoots"—birds that have migrated too far north. The Kentucky Warbler could be called the "Elvis warbler" because of the male's impressive sideburns and lovely voice. Its loud song sounds like *"Cheery, cheery, cheery, cheery,"* similar to the song of a Mourning Warbler but without a drop at the end. And like the Mourning Warbler, the Kentucky Warbler is often found foraging on the ground. The best places to find it are spring migration hot spots, such as Pelee Island, Point Pelee National Park, Rondeau Provincial Park, and Long Point Provincial Park.

Male has yellow eyebrow that wraps behind eye, black crown and sideburns, olive-green upperparts, and yellow underparts. Legs pink. No tail spots. Female similar but with mottled black on crown.

Common Yellowthroat

Paruline masquée

Geothlypis trichas

L 11–13 CM (4–5 IN) | **WS** 15–20 CM (6–8 IN)

Sporting a crisp black mask, the energetic male Common Yellowthroat resembles a tiny Lone Ranger or Zorro. The mask-less female is trickier to identify. Note how the yellow of her throat and breast blends into the dingy white of her belly and back to the bright yellow of her undertail coverts. Common Yellowthroats are found in many wet, densely vegetated habitats across the province. They are easiest to see when a male sings from an exposed cattail. The song is a distinctive *witchity, witchity, witchity, witch!*

Male has black mask bordered with white, yellow throat and breast, and whitish or buffy belly. Undertail coverts yellow. Upperparts dull olive. No tail spots.

Female lacks or has very little black or white on face and suggestion of light eyebrow and eye ring. (First-winter male similar but with hint of dark mask.)

Hooded Warbler

Paruline à capuchon

Setophaga citrina

L 13 CM (5 IN) | **WS** 17–18 CM (7 IN)

Found mostly in the Carolinian zone, the "balaclava warbler" was listed as Threatened in Ontario in 1994 but deemed Not at Risk after recent population increases, a rare victory. Found in large forests with gaps in the canopy, Hooded Warblers nest in small trees and shrubs that grow where sunlight reaches the understory. The amount of black on the female's head ranges from none to almost male-like; scientists are unsure why this variation occurs. The warbler's sweet, rich song sounds like *weety weety weety-a-oo*, similar in pattern to the Magnolia Warbler's song but made with a more musical, clear whistle.

Male has black hood, yellow forehead and cheeks, olive-green back and rump, and yellow underparts. Tail spots white. Legs pinkish.

Female similar, but black in hood varies. Usually has some yellow on chin and greenish feathers in nape.

American Redstart

Paruline flamboyante

Setophaga ruticilla

L 11–13 cm (4–5 in) | **WS** 16–20 cm (6–8 in)

The American Redstart is both easy and difficult to identify. The male's black body and bright orange patches, and the female's grey head and yellow flashes, are quickly recognizable, but the redstart's song can be tricky. It has to be learned by quality as opposed to a regular pattern. It often, but certainly not always, ends with a down-slurred note. The warbler breeds in young open forests and forest edges from southern Ontario north to the southern edge of the Hudson Bay Lowlands.

Male black with orange at base of wing and tail feathers and on sides of breast. Belly and undertail coverts white.

First-year male and female have grey head with thin, broken, whitish eye ring and yellowish patches where adult male has orange. (First-year male may have small black spots on face and breast.)

Blackburnian Warbler

Paruline à gorge orangée

Setophaga fusca

L 10-12 CM (4-5 IN) | **WS** 20-23 CM (8-9 IN)

Striking black, orange, and white feathers make the American
Redstart and Blackburnian Warbler the "Halloween warblers."
The male Blackburnian's breast is so brilliant it seems as if a
bright light is shining from inside. The warbler is associated
with eastern hemlocks but likes other conifer species as well.
Older birders who have lost the upper range of their hearing
may be unable to hear the warbler's song, a series of very high
notes, the last of which slurs upwards and almost disappears:
seat seat seat ti-ti-ti zeeeee.

Male has black crown
and cheek, orange
eyebrow, throat, partial
eye ring, and hindcheek,
and white wing patch.
Orange breast fades to
yellow towards belly.
Black streaks on sides.
Belly and undertail
coverts white or very
light yellow. Back black
with whitish lines. Large
white spots in tail.

Female similar, but
yellowish orange replaces
orange and brownish
grey replaces black. Two
white wing bars. Back
streaked.

Yellow-throated Warbler

Paruline à gorge jaune

Setophaga dominica

L 13–15 CM (5–6 IN) | **WS** 20–21 CM (8 IN)

Like the Worm-eating Warbler and the Kentucky Warbler, the
Yellow-throated Warbler is found in Ontario only occasionally,
usually after it has overshot its breeding range while migrating
in spring and stopped along the north shore of Lake Erie and
Lake Ontario. Rare bird alerts and eBird can let you know
when one is around. The warbler's song is a series of thin down-
slurred whistles that descends in pitch and is similar in quality
to the Indigo Bunting's song.

Striking, with bluish-grey upperparts,
triangular black cheek patch, bright
yellow throat and breast, white eyebrow,
and partial white eye ring. White patch
behind cheek and two white wing bars.

Kirtland's Warbler

Paruline de Kirtland

Setophaga kirtlandii

L 13–15 CM (5–6 IN) | **WS** 22–23 CM (9 IN)

The Kirtland's Warbler is one of the rarest songbirds in North
America. Its population dropped to only 201 singing males
(all in Michigan) in 1987 but has since been brought back to
over 2,300 pairs, thanks to painstaking forest management
and determined cowbird control. The warbler now breeds in
Wisconsin as well as Michigan, and it has nested in Ontario, at
Canadian Forces Base Petawawa, near Algonquin Provincial
Park. The recovery stirs hopes that birders in the province will
someday be able to observe the bird on its breeding territory
as well as during migration. The warbler appears annually in
spring at parks such as Point Pelee, Rondeau, and Long Point.
Song is a fluid series of rich notes similar in quality to the song
of the Northern Waterthrush.

Bluish-grey dark-streaked
upperparts and yellow throat, breast,
and belly with black streaks or spots
on sides. Two thin white wing bars.
Undertail coverts white. Pumps tail
constantly. (Female duller.)

Cape May Warbler

Paruline tigrée

Setophaga tigrina

L 12–13 CM (5 IN) | **WS** 20–22 CM (8–9 IN)

The Cape May Warbler's population density in a given breeding
area is often directly related to the bird's main summer food
source, the spruce budworm. In the early 1980s, the density of
Cape Mays in northern Ontario was estimated to be 370 pairs
per square kilometer, but the number dropped to close to zero
in a low budworm season a few years later. The bird's clutch size
ranges from four to nine, with an average of six, the largest of any
warbler, and it is the only warbler with a semi-tubular tongue. The
adaptation enables it to add nectar to its diet while on its winter
grounds. Listen for a very high-pitched *seet seet seet seet seet*.

Male has blackish crown and eye line, distinctive
chestnut cheek patch, yellow throat and collar,
and black-streaked yellow breast. Back olive
green with black spots. Rump yellow. White wing
patch. White tail spots.

Female greyish green with grey cheek patch,
yellowish throat, pale yellow patch behind
cheeks, and pale yellow breast and sides streaked
with grey. Rump yellowish. Thin whitish wing bars.
(First-spring and first-fall female can be very
dull.)

Prairie Warbler

Paruline des prés

Setophaga discolor

L 10-13 CM (4-5 IN) | **WS** 18 CM (7 IN)

The Prairie Warbler's main population in Ontario is found along the east shore of Georgian Bay, where, despite its name, the warbler feels quite at home amid the scattered trees and shrubs on the barren Canadian Shield rock. In other areas, the Prairie Warbler uses early successional habitats with open canopy and scrubby woody plants. The province's entire population in the mid-2000s was estimated to be only about 300 pairs. The warbler's song is a distinctive series of buzzing notes that ascend in pitch, as if the bird were practicing scales in a music lesson.

Male has yellow face with black eye line and semicircle under eye, olive-green crown and upperparts with chestnut streaks on back, and yellow underparts with black streaks on sides. Large white tail spots.

Female similar, but most or all facial markings olive green. Less chestnut on back, less black streaking on breast.

Cerulean Warbler

Paruline azurée

Setophaga cerulea

L 10-13 cm (4-5 in) | **WS** 18-20 cm (7-8 in)

The male Cerulean Warbler appears like he is wearing a coat made of a piece of the sky. But seeing his colours is tricky, since he and the bluish-green female spend most of their time at the tops of trees in dense deciduous forests. As well, the species is Endangered in Ontario, so we don't have that many Ceruleans to find. Some of the best places to look for them in their breeding habitat include Lambton County Heritage Forest, Backus Woods, and the Frontenac Arch (east of Kingston). Song is a buzzy series of notes that rise in pitch at the end: *zray zray zray zuh-zuh-zuh-zreeeeeeeee!* Be careful not to confuse it with the song of our other blue warbler, the Black-throated Blue.

Male has bright blue upperparts, white underparts with dark bluish band across breast, dark streaks on sides, and two white wing bars. White spots in tail.

Female has light turquoise upperparts with bluer crown, white or buffy eyebrow, and pale yellow underparts with indistinct blurry streaks on sides. Wing bars whitish. (First-spring females may be greener.)

Black-throated Blue Warbler

Paruline bleue

Setophaga caerulescens

L 10–13 cm (4–5 in) | **WS** 18–20 cm (7–8 in)

The plumage worn by the male and female Black-throated Blue Warbler differs dramatically, more than in any other warbler species. The male's navy upperparts, black face and throat, and white underparts are sure to grab any birder's attention, while the best identifying features of the brownish-green female are a subtle eye line, a whitish eyebrow, and a small patch of white at the base of the primary feathers. (This so-called handkerchief appears on the male's wings, too.) The Black-throated Blue Warbler's buzzy song sounds like *"I am so lay-zee."*

Male has blue upperparts, black face, throat, and sides, and white wing patch, underparts, and tail spots.

Female has brownish-green upperparts, buffy underparts, whiter on belly and undertail coverts, thin light eyebrow, and broken eye ring. First-fall female may lack white "handkerchief."

Northern Parula

Paruline à collier

Setophaga americana

L 10–12 CM (4–5 IN) | **WS** 16–18 CM (6–7 IN)

If you watch a Northern Parula as it hangs in different positions while foraging, you will see why warblers were once thought to be related to chickadees and titmice and how this warbler got its common name. (The word parula means "little chickadee.") During the breeding season, it often uses forests containing trees festooned with one of the abundant lichens in the genus *Usnea*, building its nests inside the tangled mass of lichen threads. Its buzzy song rises and then falls sharply: *zee-up!*

Male has blue head, back, and rump, olive-green triangle on back, yellow throat and breast with sunset-like band of black and chestnut, and bold white wing bars. Belly and undertail coverts white. White tail spots.

Female duller. Fall bird especially dull, lacks breast band.

Chestnut-sided Warbler

Paruline à flancs marron

Setophaga pensylvanica

L 12-15 cm (5-6 in) | **WS** 19-21 cm (7-8 in)

Looking at throat colour can help you tell this warbler from the Bay-breasted Warbler, which also has brownish sides: In summer, its throat is gleaming white, while the throat of the Bay-breasted is dark. In winter, a grey face and white eye ring replaces the Chestnut-sided's black mask and white cheeks, and it also shows much less of its namesake chestnut sides. The Chestnut-sided Warbler's whistled songs can be similar to the Yellow Warbler's song, sounding like *"Pleased pleased pleased to meetcha!"*

Male has yellow crown, black mask, white cheeks, and white underparts. Broad chestnut line runs from breast to flanks. Back greenish with black streaks. Yellowish wing bars. White tail spots. (Female duller, especially on face and the amount of chestnut on sides.)

Fall bird has lime-green crown and back, grey face, and white eye ring. Still may have some chestnut on sides.

Bay-breasted Warbler

Paruline à poitrine baie

Setophaga castanea

L 13-15 CM (5-6 IN) | **WS** 20-22 CM (8-9 IN)

Large and chunky, the Bay-breasted doesn't always move in the
hyperactive fashion of other warblers. It breeds in the boreal
forest and, like the Cape May Warbler, is a spruce budworm
specialist whose population increases during outbreaks and
decreases when the insect is absent. In fall, the Bay-breasted
Warbler's plumage closely matches that of the Blackpoll
Warbler and the Pine Warbler, making the three species tricky
to tell apart during migration. The Bay-breasted sings a high-
pitched up-and-down song similar to a Black-and-white
Warbler, though sometimes the notes are all on one pitch.

Male in spring has black mask, reddish-
chestnut crown, throat, breast, and sides,
and buffy patch behind cheek. Back grey
with black streaks and two bold white
wing bars. Legs dark. White spots in tail.

Fall bird has olive crown, dusky lores and eye line, and indistinct yellowish eyebrow. Buffy undertail coverts. May have some chestnut on throat, crown, and/or sides.

Female similar but has less chestnut in crown and buffy or whitish cheeks with dark mottling. Throat may be whitish or light chestnut. Light chestnut on sides and breast. Back has olive tinge and less streaking.

Blackpoll Warbler

Paruline rayée

Setophaga striata

L 13-15 cm (5-6 in) | **WS** 21-23 cm (8-9 in)

This warbler breeds in the province in the northern boreal forest and the Hudson Bay Lowlands and is one of the last warblers to move through southern Ontario in spring, appearing in late May or even early June. Its fall migration is very impressive: the bird travels to the east coast from as far away as Alaska and then flies non-stop for up to three and a half days over the Atlantic Ocean to northern Brazil. To fuel its journey, it almost doubles its body weight before departure. The Blackpoll Warbler tends to stick to the treetops, so knowing its song is important. Listen for a very high and fast series of thin, evenly pitched notes.

Male has black cap and moustache and white cheeks. Underparts white with black streaks on sides. Upperparts grey with black streaks. White wing bars. Legs usually yellow or pinkish in spring. White tail spots.

Fall birds have blurry dark eyeline, yellowish eyebrow, white wing bars and often pale legs. White undertail coverts contrast with usually yellowish underparts.

Female has greyish crown and upperparts, dusky eye line, light eyebrow, black streaks on back, and white wing bars. Blurry moustache may be present. Underparts white or yellowish with thin streaks on sides and, sometimes, breast. Legs yellow or pinkish.

Yellow Warbler

Paruline jaune

Setophaga petechia

L 12–13 CM (5 IN) | **WS** 16–20 CM (6–8 IN)

The common Yellow Warbler can be found throughout the province during the breeding season. It prefers scrubby or early succession habitats and often occurs along rivers. Its nest is a frequent target of the Brown-headed Cowbird, a nest parasite. The warbler isn't capable of ejecting the cowbird's eggs, so it pursues another strategy: it buries each egg under a new nest. If additional cowbird eggs appear, the warbler continues to build on top of them. One nest was found that had six layers covering 11 cowbird eggs. It ended up 14.6 cm (5.75 in) high. The Yellow Warbler's song is a high, clear whistle sounding like *"Sweet sweet shredded wheat!"*

Male all yellow with plain face, greenish-yellow neck, back, and rump, and red streaks on breast and sides. Wing feathers greenish yellow, edged in yellow. Yellow spots in tail.

Female similar but with greenish-yellow crown and little or no red on breast.

Palm Warbler

Paruline à couronne rousse

Setophaga palmarum

L 12–14 cm (5–6 in) | **WS** 20–21 cm (8 in)

The Palm Warbler is an early spring migrant in southern
Ontario. Despite its southern-sounding name, it breeds in the
province primarily in the bogs and fens of the remote boreal
forest and Hudson Bay Lowlands, although a small population
also nests near Ottawa. Taxonomists recognize two subspecies,
which can be separated by plumage, especially in spring. Most
of Ontario's Palms belong to the widespread "Western" subspecies, identifiable by their pale dirty white bellies. The warblers
that breed near Ottawa include members of the eastern or
"Yellow" subspecies, whose underparts are much yellower. Palm
Warblers sing a weak and wavering trill.

"Western" has chestnut crown, yellowish
eyebrow, dark eye line, yellow throat,
greyish-brown back, and pale breast and
belly. Breast and sides streaked with reddish
chestnut. Undertail coverts yellow. (Fall
warbler greyish brown and faintly streaked.)

"Yellow" similar but with brighter yellow
eyebrow, full yellow underparts, and
redder streaks on breast.

Pine Warbler

Paruline des pins

Setophaga pinus

L 13-15 CM (5-6 IN) | **WS** 19-23 CM (7-9 IN)

Any birder who hears a Chipping Sparrow-like trill in a pine plantation or mixed woodland should consider that the singer might be a Pine Warbler. The songs of the two birds sound very similar. Rarely seen away from pines, the Pine Warbler is the only warbler known to eat seeds regularly. It does this mostly in winter, and its digestive tract changes in this season to accommodate seed digestion. This habit makes the Pine Warbler, unlike most warblers, likely to visit a feeder (where it may also eat suet). The bird comes to Ontario feeders mostly in spring but has done so in winter, too.

Male has olive-green crown and cheek, broken yellow eye ring, yellow throat, and olive-green back and rump. Breast yellow with variable dusky streaks on sides.

Female similar but not as bright, has less yellow on breast and usually no streaks on sides. First-spring warbler (shown) and first-fall female can be very brownish.

Black-throated Green Warbler

Paruline à gorge noire

Setophaga virens

L 10-12 cm (4-5 in) | **WS** 17-20 cm (7-8 in)

Even non-birders can pick out the buzzy song of the Black-throated Green Warbler, issued high in the treetops. *"It's meeee black and green!"* the warbler seems to say. It sings two distinctive raspy songs: it usually sings *zee zee zoo-zoo zee* to attract, or communicate with, a mate, while it sings *zee zee zee zoo zee* in territorial interactions with other males. The Black-throated Green Warbler nests in all regions containing suitable mature forests with large conifers.

Male has yellow face, dusky cheeks, black throat, olive-green back and rump, and white wing bars. Black streaks on sides of breast. Belly white, sometimes yellowish. Undertail coverts white. Large white tail spots.

Female similar but with whitish throat and less and variable amounts of black on breast.

Yellow-rumped Warbler

Paruline à croupion jaune

Setophaga coronata

L 12–14 cm (5–6 in) | **WS** 19–23 cm (7–9 in)

The Magnolia Warbler, Cape May Warbler, and Yellow-rumped Warbler all have bright yellow rumps, but only the Yellow-rumped is affectionately known as "butterbutt." One of Ontario's most commonly seen warblers, it breeds across the province where mature coniferous and mixed forests occur and is often one of the first warblers seen in spring and the last warbler to leave in fall. Some Yellow-rumpeds even stay for the winter in the extreme south. The species name *coronata* means "crowned" and refers to a little patch of yellow on the crown. The warbler's song is a weak series of warbled notes that usually gets softer at the end.

Male has bluish-grey upperparts, black cheeks, broken white eye ring, white throat, yellow patches on sides of breast, and yellow rump. Wing bars and tail spots white. Female duller.

Fall warbler similar but browner, with duller eyebrow, broken eye ring, and buffy wash on breast. Wings can conceal yellow rump.

Magnolia Warbler

Paruline à tête cendrée

Setophaga magnolia

L 11–13 cm (4–5 in) | **WS** 16–20 cm (6–8 in)

Like the Yellow-rumped Warbler, the male Magnolia Warbler combines black, grey, yellow, and white, but throat colour saves the day: The Magnolia has a yellow throat, while the Yellow-rumped has a white throat (although Yellow-rumpeds out west do have a yellow throat). Note also that the Magnolia's tail spots stop abruptly halfway down the tail, making the tip look like it was dipped in ink. This field mark is easy to see and works on all ages and plumages, and it is especially useful in autumn, when colours can be very dull and confusing. The Magnolia Warbler sings a soft *weety weety weety-o*, somewhat similar but less musical than the song of a Hooded Warbler.

Male has black cheeks, white eyebrow (behind eye only), mostly black back with large white wing patch, and yellow throat, breast, and belly with "necklace" of thick black streaks.

Female duller with greyer cheeks and olive-green back with black spots. Fall warbler can be even duller.

Canada Warbler

Paruline du Canada

Cardellina canadensis

L 12–15 CM (5–6 IN) | **WS** 17–22 CM (7–9 IN)

Once listed as Threatened in Ontario, the Canada Warbler is now considered a species of Special Concern, meaning it is not in as much trouble as it once was. The greyish-blue and yellow warbler looks like a Magnolia Warbler without all the extra bling. Its best field marks are a black "necklace," white undertail coverts, and an absence of wing bars. One of the only warblers that might truly be thought to warble, the Canada Warbler starts its song with a sharp chip, then whistles a jumble of varied fluid notes. Knowing the song is crucial to finding the warbler in densely vegetated wet mixed forests.

Male has greyish-blue upperparts, yellow throat and belly, and white undertail coverts. Yellow eyebrow joins yellow or whitish eye ring to make "spectacles." Black streaks on breast form "necklace."

Female warbler similar but duller. "Necklace" may be indistinct or lacking.

Wilson's Warbler

Paruline à calotte noire

Cardellina pusilla

L 10-12 CM (4-5 IN) | **WS** 14-17 CM (5-7 IN)

The Wilson's Warbler breeds in Ontario in the boreal forest and Hudson Bay Lowlands, where it builds a cup-shaped nest on the ground in forest edges and willow, alder, and shrubby thickets near streams. The female looks remarkably similar to the female Yellow Warbler. To tell them apart, study the Wilson's tail — it's longer in proportion to body size than the Yellow's tail — and note that the Wilson's wings are plain, not edged in yellow, as the Yellow's wings are. The male Wilson's Warbler sings a loud, sharp, slow trill that may drop in pitch and/or speed up at the end.

Male has olive-green upperparts, yellow underparts, yellow face, and black cap. No tail spots.

Female similar but with olive or small black cap.

Summer Tanager

Piranga vermillon
Piranga rubra

L 16–18 CM (6–7 IN) | **WS** 28–30 CM (11–12 IN)

The Summer Tanager breeds in forests in the eastern and southern United States but usually shows up in Ontario annually. The male's all-red plumage distinguishes it from the male Scarlet Tanager's crimson body and black wings. Female tanagers are trickier to tell apart, since each is olive green and yellowish; watch for the Summer's larger beak and lighter wings and tail. The first-spring male Summer Tanager can look like a greenish-yellow and red patchwork quilt. The song is like an American Robin's song but with a few raspy notes.

Male all red with strong pale beak.

Female has olive-yellow upperparts and dull yellow or orangish-yellow underparts. (First-spring male similar but with variable red patches.)

Scarlet Tanager

Piranga écarlate

Piranga olivacea

L 16-17 CM (6-7 IN) | **WS** 25-30 CM (10-12 IN)

Seeing a bright red male Scarlet Tanager high in a leafy canopy may make you think that some exquisite species from a tropical rainforest has become really lost. In fact, many tanager species can be found in Central and South America, but the Scarlet Tanager only overwinters there. Its breeding range in Ontario extends from the extreme south to the southern edge of the boreal forest. The tanager can be surprisingly hard to spot, despite its glowing plumage; its song, somewhat like that of an American Robin with a sore throat, will help you find it.

Male brilliant crimson (rarely orange) with black wings and tail. Beak grey.

Female olive green with dusky wings and tail. Beak pale.

Northern Cardinal

Cardinal rouge

Cardinalis cardinalis

L 21–23 cm (8–9 in) | **WS** 25–31 cm (10–12 in)

All birdwatchers want this bird in their backyard. And more and more people in the southern part of Ontario are getting their wish, as the species expands northward. Believe it or not, it was not always in the province. The first record was in 1849, and the first nest was found at Point Pelee in 1901. Now the Northern Cardinal occurs as far north as Timmins, Thunder Bay, and Rainy River. The male's red is stunning, but the female's rich ochre is just as pretty. Song is a series of fluid, clear notes sounding like *"Niiiice briiiight reeeed birdy-birdy-birdy-birdy-birdy."* Call is a sharp *pick*.

Male all red with large crest, black face, red or orange beak, and long rounded tail. Back greyish red.

Female warm brown with reddish crest, wings, and tail, blackish face, and orange beak. Long, rounded tail.

Rose-breasted Grosbeak

Cardinal à poitrine rose

Pheucticus ludovicianus

L 18–21 CM (7–8 IN)   **WS** 29–33 CM (11–13 IN)

"There is a giant sparrow at my feeder!" This is often the reaction when someone sees a female Rose-breasted Grosbeak for the first time. Its markings and shape are very reminiscent of a sparrow or finch, but the bird is just too big. Her mate is much easier to identify, with his black and white plumage and flashy red breast patch. The Rose-breasted Grosbeak is a summer visitor to Ontario, found from Essex County north to the boreal forest. The rich whistle sounds like the song of an American Robin that has taken music lessons.

Male has black head and back, white underparts, red triangle on breast, and large pink beak. Rump and wing patches white. (First-summer male has brownish-white feathers and may have less black and red than older male.)

Female has brown head and back, with white eyebrow and throat, streaked breast and sides, and large pink beak. Wing bars white.

Indigo Bunting

Passerin indigo

Passerina cyanea

L 12–13 CM (5 IN) | **WS** 19–22 CM (7–9 IN)

Viewed in the right light, the blue of the male Indigo Bunting may seem just too tropical for Ontario. There's nothing like having a flock of lemon-yellow goldfinches and a bunting or two share a feeder in spring. Buntings studied in a planetarium helped scientists figure out that birds were using the stars to help determine their direction for migration. The Indigo Bunting breeds mostly in southern parts of the province, preferring open habitats such as hedgerows, clearings under hydro lines, and forest edges. Its song is a series of paired phrases, often described as *"Fire, fire, where, where, there, there, put it out."*

Male brilliant blue. Beak grey.

Female light brown above and pale brown below, with pale throat and faint blue highlights in wings and tail. Faint blurry streaks on breast. Winter and first-spring male similar but may have varying amounts of blue patches.

Dickcissel

Dickcissel d'Amérique

Spiza americana

L 13-16 CM (5-6 IN) | **WS** 25-26 CM (10 IN)

The core of the Dickcissel's regular breeding range is in the
midwestern United States, but occasionally, usually during
drought years, it irrupts, moving unpredictably into new areas,
including in Ontario. One of the province's rarest and most
inconsistent breeding birds, it often chooses large areas of tall
grasses and other herbaceous plants. The male sings up to 70
percent of the day when establishing a territory. His song is
often described as an insect-like *dick dick ciss ciss ciss*.

Male has grey head, yellowish
eyebrow, rufous shoulder patch,
and yellow breast marked with
black V. Sides greyish. Belly and
undertail coverts white.

Adult female similar but
browner, lacks breast patch,
and has less rufous on wings.
(First-winter female can be
much duller.)

Acknowledgments

There have been so many influential people during my decades of birding that it would be impossible to list them all. I thank friends who birded with me; family members who listened to me talk about birds non-stop; teachers and professors who opened doors of knowledge; and all of my workshop participants, undergrad/graduate students and visiting school children whose interest and questions kept me on my toes. I would also like to acknowledge you, the reader. You are the one who can make a difference for the continued existence of our natural spaces. Thank you for being curious about the beings on our planet.

It has been a pleasure, once again, to work with Brian Small. From my very first bird book in 1999, Brian has been supportive and friendly throughout all of my projects. By sharing his incredible craft of capturing birds and their lives in photos he has made a difference in conserving our feathered friends. Thanks also to my other long-time photographers, Tony Beck, Karl Egressy, Scott Fairbairn, Robert McCaw and John Reaume for their talent, continued support and friendship. I appreciate the wonderful images of the other photographers, in this book, too –keep up the great work!

George Scott, I appreciate your patience and encouragement throughout this project and I am thrilled to be a part of the quality works in the ABA state/provincial book series. These books and the meaning they bring to naturalists across the continent would not be possible without publishers like yourself.

Scott & Nix Acknowledgments

Many thanks to Nikki Belmonte, Ted Floyd, John Lowry, Nathan Swick, Kelly Smith, and everyone at the American Birding Association for their good work. Thanks to Alan Poole, Miyoko Chu, and especially Kevin J. McGowan at the Cornell Lab of Ornithology for their bird measurement data sets. We give special thanks to Brian E. Small, and all the other contributors for their extraordinary photographs in the guide. We thank Chuck Hagner for his work on the manuscript; Eli Van Belle for layout help; James Montalbano of Terminal Design for his typefaces; Charles Nix for the series design; and René Porter Nedelkoff of the Porter Print Group.

Image Credits

(T) = Top, (B) = Bottom, (L) = Left, (R) = Right; pages with multiple images from one source are indicated by a single credit.

XIII– XXXV Brian E. Small. 2–16 Brian E. Small. 17 Tony Beck (T), Brian E. Small(). 18–38 Brian E. Small. 39 Robert McCaw. 40 Brian E. Small. 41 Karl Egressy. 41–44 Brian E. Small. 45 Brian E. Small(T), Joe Fuhrman(B). 46–52 Brian E. Small. 53 Jacob S. Spendelow. 54–69 Brian E. Small. 70 Brian E. Small(T), Robert McCaw (B). 71–85 Brian E. Small. 86 Brian E. Small(T), Robert McCaw(B). 87 Brian E. Small. 88 Garth McElroy. 89–96 Brian E. Small. 97 Brian E. Small (T), Mike Danzenbaker (B). 98 Brian E. Small (L), Darlene Friedman (R). 99 Tony Beck. 100 Tony Beck (T), Joe Fuhrman(B). 101–102 Brian E. Small. 103 Tony Beck(T), Alan Murphy(B). 104 Mike Danzenbaker. 105 Glen Bartley. 106 Brian E. Small. 109 Brian E. Small(T), Robert McCaw(B). 110–113 Brian E. Small. 114 Tony Beck (L), Brian E. Small (R). 115 Scott Fairbairn(T), Brian E. Small(B). 116 Justin Peter (T), Tony Beck (B). 117–136 Brian E. Small. 137 Jerry Liguori. 138–139 Brian E. Small. 140 Jim Zipp(T), Alan Murphy(B). 141 Alan Murphy. 142 Brian E. Small. 143 Brian E. Small (T), Jim Zipp (B). 144 Jim Zipp. 145–146 Brian E. Small. 147 Paul Konrad (L), Brian E. Small (R). 148–153 Brian E. Small. 154 Jacob S. Spendelow. 155–157 Brian E. Small. 158 Brian E. Small(L), Alan Murphy(R). 159–162 Brian E. Small. 163 John Reaume (), Scott Fairbairn (R). 164–168 Brian E. Small. 169 Brian E. Small (L), Jim Zipp (R). 170 Brian E. Small. 171 Robert McCaw (T), Tony Beck (B). 172–189 Brian E. Small. 190 Jim Zipp. 191–197 Brian E. Small. 198 Brian E. Small (L), 198 Ben Bartley/VIREO (R). 199–216 Brian E. Small. 217 Robert McCaw. 218–232 Brian E. Small. 233 Jacob Spendelow. 234–240 Brian E. Small. 241 Brian E. Small(T), Robert McCaw (B). 242 Brian E. Small. 243 Robert McCaw. 244–247 Brian E. Small. 248 Karl Egressy. 249–260 Brian E. Small. 261 Brian E. Small (T), Alan Murphy (B). 262 Brian E. Small (T), Jacob S. Spendelow (B). 263–284 Brian E. Small. 285 Brian E. Small(T), Judy M. Tomlinson(B). 286–298 Brian E. Small. 299 Brian E. Small(T), Rob Curtis/VIREO(B). 300–302 Brian E. Small. 303 Robert McCaw. 304–307 Brian E. Small. 308 Brian E. Small(T), Alan Murphy(B). 309 Brian E. Small. 310 Brian E. Small(T), Alan Murphy(B). 311–317 Brian E. Small.

Checklist of the Birds of Ontario

This list has been adapted from the Ontario Field Ornithologists and comprises 508 bird species that have been recorded in Ontario on the basis of specimens, photographs, recordings and documented sight records accepted by the Ontario Bird Records Committee (OBRC). A total of 291 species is known to have bred in the province. Classification and nomenclature follow the American Ornithologists' Union *Checklist of North American Birds*, (7th Edition, 1998) and its 42nd–62nd (2021) supplements. Please note that pocket-sized Ontario checklists are available for purchase at ofo.ca. Species names in the list preceeded with an asterix (*) indicates it has been recorded as breeding in Ontario.

Ducks, Geese, and Waterfowl

☐ Black-bellied Whistling-Duck
☐ Fulvous Whistling-Duck
☐ *Snow Goose
☐ *Ross's Goose
☐ Greater White-fronted Goose
☐ Tundra Bean-Goose
☐ Pink-footed Goose
☐ Brant
☐ Barnacle Goose
☐ Cackling Goose
☐ *Canada Goose
☐ *Mute Swan
☐ *Trumpeter Swan
☐ *Tundra Swan
☐ *Wood Duck
☐ Garganey
☐ *Blue-winged Teal
☐ *Cinnamon Teal
☐ *Northern Shoveler
☐ *Gadwall
☐ Eurasian Wigeon
☐ *American Wigeon
☐ *Mallard
☐ *American Black Duck
☐ Mottled Duck
☐ *Northern Pintail
☐ *Green-winged Teal
☐ *Canvasback
☐ *Redhead
☐ *Ring-necked Duck
☐ Tufted Duck
☐ *Greater Scaup
☐ *Lesser Scaup
☐ *King Eider
☐ *Common Eider
☐ Harlequin Duck
☐ *Surf Scoter
☐ *White-winged Scoter
☐ *Black Scoter
☐ *Long-tailed Duck
☐ *Bufflehead
☐ *Common Goldeneye
☐ Barrow's Goldeneye
☐ Smew
☐ *Hooded Merganser
☐ *Common Merganser
☐ *Red-breasted Merganser
☐ *Ruddy Duck

New World Quail

☐ *Northern Bobwhite

Pheasants, Grouse, and Allies

☐ *Gray Partridge
☐ *Ring-necked Pheasant
☐ *Ruffed Grouse
☐ *Spruce Grouse
☐ *Willow Ptarmigan
☐ Rock Ptarmigan
☐ *Sharp-tailed Grouse
☐ *Greater Prairie-Chicken
☐ *Wild Turkey

Grebes

☐ *Pied-billed Grebe
☐ *Horned Grebe
☐ *Red-necked Grebe
☐ *Eared Grebe
☐ Western Grebe

Pigeons and Doves

☐ *Rock Pigeon
☐ White-crowned Pigeon
☐ Band-tailed Pigeon
☐ Eurasian Collared-Dove
☐ *Passenger Pigeon (Extinct)
☐ Inca Dove
☐ Common Ground Dove
☐ White-winged Dove
☐ *Mourning Dove

Cuckoos

☐ Groove-billed Ani
☐ *Yellow-billed Cuckoo
☐ *Black-billed Cuckoo

Nightjars and Allies

☐ Lesser Nighthawk
☐ *Common Nighthawk
☐ Common Poorwill

☐ *Chuck-will's-widow
☐ *Eastern Whip-poor-will

Swifts

☐ Black Swift
☐ White-collared Swift
☐ *Chimney Swift

Hummingbirds

☐ Mexican Violetear
☐ *Ruby-throated Hummingbird
☐ Black-chinned Hummingbird
☐ Anna's Hummingbird
☐ Costa's Hummingbird
☐ Rufous Hummingbird
☐ Calliope Hummingbird
☐ Broad-billed Hummingbird

Rails, Gallinules, and Coots

☐ *Yellow Rail
☐ Black Rail
☐ *King Rail
☐ *Virginia Rail
☐ *Sora
☐ Purple Gallinule
☐ *Common Gallinule
☐ *American Coot

Cranes

☐ *Sandhill Crane
☐ Whooping Crane

Stilts and Avocets

☐ *Black-necked Stilt
☐ *American Avocet

Oystercatchers

☐ American Oystercatcher

Plovers and Lapwings

☐ Black-bellied Plover
☐ *American Golden-Plover
☐ Eurasian Dotterel
☐ *Killdeer
☐ Common Ringed Plover
☐ *Semipalmated Plover
☐ *Piping Plover
☐ Lesser Sand-Plover
☐ Wilson's Plover
☐ Snowy Plover

Sandpipers and Allies

☐ *Upland Sandpiper
☐ *Whimbrel
☐ Eskimo Curlew
☐ Long-billed Curlew
☐ Slender-billed Curlew
☐ Black-tailed Godwit
☐ *Hudsonian Godwit
☐ *Marbled Godwit
☐ Ruddy Turnstone
☐ Red Knot
☐ Ruff
☐ Sharp-tailed Sandpiper
☐ *Stilt Sandpiper
☐ Curlew Sandpiper
☐ Sanderling
☐ *Dunlin
☐ Purple Sandpiper
☐ Baird's Sandpiper
☐ Little Stint
☐ *Least Sandpiper
☐ White-rumped Sandpiper
☐ Buff-breasted Sandpiper
☐ *Pectoral Sandpiper
☐ *Semipalmated Sandpiper
☐ Western Sandpiper
☐ *Short-billed Dowitcher
☐ Long-billed Dowitcher
☐ *American Woodcock
☐ *Wilson's Snipe
☐ *Spotted Sandpiper
☐ *Solitary Sandpiper
☐ Wandering Tattler
☐ *Lesser Yellowlegs
☐ Willet
☐ Spotted Redshank
☐ *Greater Yellowlegs
☐ Marsh Sandpiper
☐ *Wilson's Phalarope
☐ *Red-necked Phalarope
☐ Red Phalarope

Skuas and Jaegers

☐ Pomarine Jaeger
☐ *Parasitic Jaeger
☐ Long-tailed Jaeger

Auks, Murres, and Puffins

☐ Dovekie
☐ Thick-billed Murre
☐ Razorbill
☐ *Black Guillemot

☐ Long-billed Murrelet
☐ Ancient Murrelet
☐ Atlantic Puffin

Gulls, Terns, and Skimmers

☐ Black-legged Kittiwake
☐ Ivory Gull
☐ Sabine's Gull
☐ *Bonaparte's Gull
☐ Black-headed Gull
☐ *Little Gull
☐ Ross's Gull
☐ Laughing Gull
☐ Franklin's Gull
☐ Black-tailed Gull
☐ Heermann's Gull
☐ Common Gull
☐ Short-billed Gull
☐ *Ring-billed Gull
☐ *California Gull
☐ *Herring Gull
☐ Iceland Gull
☐ Lesser Black-backed Gull
☐ Slaty-backed Gull
☐ Glaucous-winged Gull
☐ Glaucous Gull
☐ *Great Black-backed Gull
☐ Kelp Gull
☐ Sooty Tern
☐ Least Tern
☐ *Caspian Tern
☐ *Black Tern
☐ White-winged Tern
☐ *Common Tern
☐ *Arctic Tern
☐ *Forster's Tern
☐ Royal Tern
☐ Sandwich Tern
☐ Elegant Tern
☐ Black Skimmer

Loons

☐ *Red-throated Loon
☐ *Pacific Loon
☐ *Common Loon
☐ Yellow-billed Loon

Albatrosses

☐ Yellow-nosed Albatross

Storm-petrels

☐ Wilson's Storm-Petrel

Storm-Petrels

☐ Leach's Storm-Petrel
☐ Band-rumped Storm-Petrel

Shearwaters and Petrels

☐ Northern Fulmar
☐ Black-capped Petrel
☐ Short-tailed/Sooty Shearwater
☐ Great Shearwater
☐ Manx Shearwater
☐ Audubon's Shearwater

Storks

☐ Wood Stork

Frigatebirds

☐ Magnificent Frigatebird

Boobies and Gannets

☐ Brown Booby
☐ Northern Gannet

Cormorants and Shags

☐ Neotropic Cormorant
☐ *Double-crested Cormorant
☐ Great Cormorant

Anhingas

☐ Anhinga

Pelicans

☐ *American White Pelican
☐ Brown Pelican

Herons, Egrets, and Bitterns

☐ *American Bittern
☐ *Least Bittern
☐ *Great Blue Heron
☐ *Great Egret
☐ Little Egret
☐ *Snowy Egret
☐ Little Blue Heron
☐ Tricolored Heron
☐ Reddish Egret
☐ *Cattle Egret
☐ *Green Heron
☐ *Black-crowned Night-Heron
☐ Yellow-crowned Night-Heron

Ibises and Spoonbills

☐ White Ibis
☐ Glossy Ibis
☐ White-faced Ibis
☐ Roseate Spoonbill

New World Vultures

☐ Black Vulture
☐ *Turkey Vulture

Osprey

☐ *Osprey

Hawks, Eagles, and Kites

☐ Swallow-tailed Kite
☐ *Golden Eagle
☐ *Northern Harrier
☐ *Sharp-shinned Hawk
☐ *Cooper's Hawk
☐ *Northern Goshawk
☐ *Bald Eagle
☐ Mississippi Kite
☐ *Red-shouldered Hawk
☐ *Broad-winged Hawk
☐ Swainson's Hawk
☐ *Red-tailed Hawk
☐ *Rough-legged Hawk
☐ Ferruginous Hawk

Barn-Owls

☐ *Barn Owl

Owls

☐ *Eastern Screech-Owl
☐ *Great Horned Owl
☐ Snowy Owl
☐ *Northern Hawk Owl
☐ Burrowing Owl
☐ *Barred Owl
☐ *Great Gray Owl
☐ *Long-eared Owl
☐ *Short-eared Owl
☐ *Boreal Owl
☐ *Northern Saw-whet Owl

Kingfishers

☐ *Belted Kingfisher

Woodpeckers

☐ Lewis's Woodpecker
☐ *Red-headed Woodpecker
☐ *Red-bellied Woodpecker

☐ *Yellow-bellied Sapsucker
☐ *American Three-toed Woodpecker
☐ *Black-backed Woodpecker
☐ *Downy Woodpecker
☐ *Hairy Woodpecker
☐ *Northern Flicker
☐ *Pileated Woodpecker

Falcons and Caracaras

☐ Crested Caracara
☐ *American Kestrel
☐ *Merlin
☐ Gyrfalcon
☐ *Peregrine Falcon
☐ Prairie Falcon

Tyrant Flycatchers

☐ Ash-throated Flycatcher
☐ *Great Crested Flycatcher
☐ Great Kiskadee
☐ Sulphur-bellied Flycatcher
☐ Variegated Flycatcher
☐ Tropical Kingbird
☐ Cassin's Kingbird
☐ Thick-billed Kingbird
☐ *Western Kingbird
☐ *Eastern Kingbird
☐ Gray Kingbird
☐ Scissor-tailed Flycatcher
☐ Fork-tailed Flycatcher
☐ *Olive-sided Flycatcher
☐ Western Wood-Pewee
☐ *Eastern Wood-Pewee
☐ *Yellow-bellied Flycatcher
☐ *Acadian Flycatcher
☐ *Alder Flycatcher
☐ *Willow Flycatcher
☐ *Least Flycatcher
☐ Gray Flycatcher
☐ Dusky Flycatcher
☐ *Eastern Phoebe
☐ Say's Phoebe
☐ Vermilion Flycatcher

Shrikes

☐ *Loggerhead Shrike
☐ *Northern Shrike

Vireos, Shrike-Babblers, and Erpornis

☐ Black-capped Vireo

- ☐ *White-eyed Vireo
- ☐ Bell's Vireo
- ☐ *Yellow-throated Vireo
- ☐ *Blue-headed Vireo
- ☐ Plumbeous Vireo
- ☐ *Philadelphia Vireo
- ☐ *Warbling Vireo
- ☐ *Red-eyed Vireo

Crows, Jays, and Magpies
- ☐ *Canada Jay
- ☐ *Blue Jay
- ☐ Clark's Nutcracker
- ☐ *Black-billed Magpie
- ☐ Eurasian Jackdaw
- ☐ *American Crow
- ☐ *Fish Crow
- ☐ *Common Raven

Larks
- ☐ *Horned Lark

Swallows
- ☐ *Bank Swallow
- ☐ *Tree Swallow
- ☐ Violet-green Swallow
- ☐ *Northern Rough-winged Swallow
- ☐ *Purple Martin
- ☐ *Barn Swallow
- ☐ *Cliff Swallow
- ☐ Cave Swallow

Tits, Chickadees, and Titmice
- ☐ Carolina Chickadee
- ☐ *Black-capped Chickadee
- ☐ *Boreal Chickadee
- ☐ *Tufted Titmouse

Nuthatches
- ☐ *Red-breasted Nuthatch
- ☐ *White-breasted Nuthatch

Treecreepers
- ☐ *Brown Creeper

Wrens
- ☐ Rock Wren
- ☐ *House Wren
- ☐ *Winter Wren
- ☐ *Sedge Wren

- ☐ *Marsh Wren
- ☐ *Carolina Wren
- ☐ *Bewick's Wren

Leaf Warblers
- ☐ Yellow-browed Warbler

Gnatcatchers
- ☐ *Blue-gray Gnatcatcher

Kinglets
- ☐ *Golden-crowned Kinglet
- ☐ *Ruby-crowned Kinglet

Old World Flycatchers
- ☐ Siberian Rubythroat
- ☐ Northern Wheatear

Thrushes and Allies
- ☐ *Eastern Bluebird
- ☐ Mountain Bluebird
- ☐ Townsend's Solitaire
- ☐ *Veery
- ☐ *Gray-cheeked Thrush
- ☐ Bicknell's Thrush
- ☐ *Swainson's Thrush
- ☐ *Hermit Thrush
- ☐ *Wood Thrush
- ☐ Eurasian Blackbird
- ☐ Fieldfare
- ☐ *American Robin
- ☐ Varied Thrush

Mockingbirds and Thrashers
- ☐ *Gray Catbird
- ☐ *Brown Thrasher
- ☐ Sage Thrasher
- ☐ *Northern Mockingbird

Starlings
- ☐ *European Starling

Waxwings
- ☐ *Bohemian Waxwing
- ☐ *Cedar Waxwing

Silky-flycatchers
- ☐ Phainopepla

Old World Sparrows
- ☐ *House Sparrow
- ☐ Eurasian Tree Sparrow

Wagtails and Pipits
- ☐ White Wagtail
- ☐ *American Pipit
- ☐ Sprague's Pipit

Finches, Euphonias, and Allies
- ☐ Brambling
- ☐ *Evening Grosbeak
- ☐ *Pine Grosbeak
- ☐ Gray-crowned Rosy-Finch
- ☐ *House Finch
- ☐ *Purple Finch
- ☐ Cassin's Finch
- ☐ *Common Redpoll
- ☐ *Hoary Redpoll
- ☐ *Red Crossbill
- ☐ *White-winged Crossbill
- ☐ *Pine Siskin
- ☐ Lesser Goldfinch
- ☐ *American Goldfinch

Longspurs and Snow Buntings
- ☐ *Lapland Longspur
- ☐ Chestnut-collared Longspur
- ☐ *Smith's Longspur
- ☐ McCown's Longspur
- ☐ Snow Bunting

New World Buntings and Sparrows
- ☐ Cassin's Sparrow
- ☐ Bachman's Sparrow
- ☐ *Grasshopper Sparrow
- ☐ Black-throated Sparrow
- ☐ *Lark Sparrow
- ☐ Lark Bunting
- ☐ *Chipping Sparrow
- ☐ *Clay-colored Sparrow
- ☐ *Field Sparrow
- ☐ Brewer's Sparrow
- ☐ *Fox Sparrow
- ☐ *American Tree Sparrow
- ☐ *Dark-eyed Junco
- ☐ *White-crowned Sparrow
- ☐ Golden-crowned Sparrow
- ☐ *Harris's Sparrow
- ☐ *White-throated Sparrow
- ☐ *Vesper Sparrow
- ☐ *LeConte's Sparrow

- [ ] *Nelson's Sparrow
- [ ] Baird's Sparrow
- [ ] *Henslow's Sparrow
- [ ] *Savannah Sparrow
- [ ] *Song Sparrow
- [ ] *Lincoln's Sparrow
- [ ] *Swamp Sparrow
- [ ] Green-tailed Towhee
- [ ] Spotted Towhee
- [ ] *Eastern Towhee

Yellow-breasted Chat

- [ ] *Yellow-breasted Chat

Troupials and Allies

- [ ] *Yellow-headed Blackbird
- [ ] *Bobolink
- [ ] *Eastern Meadowlark
- [ ] *Western Meadowlark
- [ ] *Orchard Oriole
- [ ] Hooded Oriole
- [ ] Bullock's Oriole
- [ ] *Baltimore Oriole
- [ ] Scott's Oriole
- [ ] *Red-winged Blackbird
- [ ] *Brown-headed Cowbird
- [ ] *Rusty Blackbird
- [ ] *Brewer's Blackbird
- [ ] *Common Grackle
- [ ] Great-tailed Grackle

New World Warblers

- [ ] *Ovenbird
- [ ] Worm-eating Warbler
- [ ] *Louisiana Waterthrush
- [ ] *Northern Waterthrush
- [ ] *Golden-winged Warbler
- [ ] *Blue-winged Warbler
- [ ] *Black-and-white Warbler
- [ ] *Prothonotary Warbler
- [ ] Swainson's Warbler
- [ ] *Tennessee Warbler
- [ ] *Orange-crowned Warbler
- [ ] *Nashville Warbler
- [ ] Virginia's Warbler
- [ ] *Connecticut Warbler
- [ ] MacGillivray's Warbler
- [ ] *Mourning Warbler
- [ ] Kentucky Warbler
- [ ] *Common Yellowthroat

- [ ] *Hooded Warbler
- [ ] *American Redstart
- [ ] *Kirtland's Warbler
- [ ] *Cape May Warbler
- [ ] *Cerulean Warbler
- [ ] *Northern Parula
- [ ] *Magnolia Warbler
- [ ] *Bay-breasted Warbler
- [ ] *Blackburnian Warbler
- [ ] *Yellow Warbler
- [ ] *Chestnut-sided Warbler
- [ ] *Blackpoll Warbler
- [ ] *Black-throated Blue Warbler
- [ ] *Palm Warbler
- [ ] *Pine Warbler
- [ ] *Yellow-rumped Warbler
- [ ] Yellow-throated Warbler
- [ ] *Prairie Warbler
- [ ] Grace's Warbler
- [ ] Black-throated Gray Warbler
- [ ] Townsend's Warbler
- [ ] Hermit Warbler
- [ ] *Black-throated Green Warbler
- [ ] *Canada Warbler
- [ ] *Wilson's Warbler
- [ ] Painted Redstart

Cardinals and Allies

- [ ] Hepatic Tanager
- [ ] Summer Tanager
- [ ] *Scarlet Tanager
- [ ] Western Tanager
- [ ] *Northern Cardinal
- [ ] Pyrrhuloxia
- [ ] *Rose-breasted Grosbeak
- [ ] Black-headed Grosbeak
- [ ] Blue Grosbeak
- [ ] Lazuli Bunting
- [ ] *Indigo Bunting
- [ ] Varied Bunting
- [ ] Painted Bunting
- [ ] *Dickcissel

Species Index

M

N

About the Contributors

© MICHELLE BELTRAN

Chris Earley is the Interpretive Biologist and Education Coordinator at the University of Guelph Arboretum. He has written five bird guides as well as eight other nature books for adults and children. Since 1999, Chris has led international nature tours all over the world for Worldwide Quest. He is a winner of the Richards Education Award from Ontario Nature and is a master bird bander. He lives in Rockwood, Ontario with his wife, Jiffy.

Brian E. Small is a full-time professional bird and nature photographer. For more than 30 years, he has traveled widely across North America to capture images of birds in their native habitats. He served as the photo editor for *Birding* magazine for 15 years. Small grew up in Los Angeles, graduated from U.C.L.A. in 1982, and still lives there today with his wife Ana, daughter Nicole, and son Tyler.

Quick Index

See the Species Index for a complete listing of all the birds in the
American Birding Association Field Guide to Birds of Ontario.